More Miracles
We Have Seen

Jack and Winona Terry

More Miracles We Have Seen
by
Jack and Winona Terry

All Scripture quotations are from the New International Version of the Bible (International Bible Society, 1984).

Cover photo of the Bolivian Andes courtesy of Caetano Lacerda and HAAP Media Ltd.

Book design and editing by David Spiech

ISBN 978-0-615-27340-2

Contents

SECTION III

MERRY MISSION STORIES
WE HAVE SEEN AND HEARD

SECTION IV

SOME MISSIONARY TONGUE TWISTERS

SECTION V

SPIRITUAL WARFARE AROUND THE WORLD

v

Foreword

James W. Tharp

"They've done it again!"

Yes, my friends, Jack and Winona Terry have come through with another great report on the mighty miracles they have seen in their ministries in Asia, South America and the Caribbean, and in the USA.

My heart has been as deeply moved on reading this second report on miracles as when I read their first book. I truly believe that outstanding miracles are a part of God's design for these last days. Why wouldn't our God want to show His mighty power for genuine miracles in the face of the contrived and deceitful miracles of the Anti-Christ?

The Apostle Paul warned us believers living in the end times: "The coming of the lawless one will be in accordance with the work of Satan displayed in all kinds of counterfeit miracles, signs and wonders, and in every sort of evil that deceives those who are perishing. They perish because they refused to love the truth and so be saved. For this reason God sends them a powerful delusion so that they will believe the lie and so that all will be condemned who have not believed the truth but have delighted in wickedness" (II Thessalonians 2:9–12).

The apostle Peter explained to his Pentecostal audience of several thousand people that "Jesus of Nazareth was a man accredited by God to you by miracles, wonders and signs, which God did among you through him, as you yourselves know" (Acts 2:22).

All through the book of Acts we see Spirit-filled apostles, deacons

Rev. James W. Tharp is a renowned evangelist who has worked closely with Rev. Billy Graham around the world. He has also led several great churches in America. One of his very fruitful ministries in recent years has been with Christian Renewal Ministries. In this life-changing ministry Evangelist Tharp has taught Prayer Seminars in many nations.

and others performing miracles—the sick recover, the lame walk, the blind receive their sight and even the dead are raised! With what results? Multitudes—saints and sinners—start to praise God! A new God-consciousness is developed! And individuals are forced to reconsider the Person and power of One in whose name the miracle took place! Jesus, the Risen Savior, is Lord! He is the Omnipotent Ruler of the universe! Therefore in the face of such miracles, mortal men are forced to deal with their relationship with Him! Will they confess Him as Lord and Savior, or will they shrug Him off and hear Him say at the Judgment, "Depart from me?"

So, dear readers, let us hear of these miracles and join the revival of praise that will increase around the world as Spirit-anointed witnesses such as Winona and Jack Terry continue to see the great miracles, signs and wonders as they travel this world preaching the Gospel and declaring that "Jesus Christ is the same yesterday and today and forever" (Hebrews 13:8).

James W. Tharp
Bozeman, Montana

More Miracles
We Have Seen

Section I
Miracle Stories

1

Mamee and Mama-san's
Miracles in Haiti

"Mama-san! Don't you think we should take some food out to the workers in Pernier?" Marlene asked Winona, early one bright, sunshiny day in Port au Prince, Haiti. We had gone to Haiti to begin the first school and church building construction. Our group consisted of Charlie Collins, Adam Bryan from Nora Christian Fellowship, plus Winona and Jack Terry.

So, Winona and Marlene decided on 5 pounds of chicken, 6 pounds of rice, and some bread and water for the cooler. They felt that this would be enough food for 14 people. Marlene also bought paper plates and cups.

When the food was completed we were all amazed that a crowd of people had gathered to watch the construction. We had a dilemma. We had prepared only enough for 14 people, but to our astonishment there were over 60 people surrounding our little makeshift outdoor kitchen.

We did not know how far the food would stretch since we had prepared for only 14 people. Our hearts were a bit heavy as we saw all those hungry people standing and looking at the food about to be dispersed to the workers and the missionaries. Marlene and the Haitian cooks began to fill paper plates with rice, chicken, bread and a cup of water. Charlie, Adam, Winona and I were willing to give our portions, but what about all the other children and adults? We prayed a blessing upon the food and all of the people gathered.

We could not believe what happened next. Soon, everyone had a full plate of rice and chicken. That included us! We counted more than 60 people gathered there that day as the workers began to build a school and church for those precious people. Then...everyone got seconds! It was a time of rejoicing! But, that was not the end of the story.

After everyone got all they wanted to eat, the young boys came to Winona and said, "Mama-san, would you like to hear our band?" Winona smiled as the boys collected plastic jugs and some pieces of metal and began to play music in a calypso style rhythm. It was full of energy and joy. When they finished the young girls came running to Winona and eagerly asked, "Don't you want to hear us sing?" In a few minutes the mountainside was echoing with the vibrant sounds of worship and praise. Then, Mamee arrived!

Mamee was the 85-year-old lady who gave the land for the new school and church. She was the reason we were there. She had prayed for six years that someone would come to her remote hillside in Haiti and open a school and church for her desperately needy neighbors. Now she was ready to celebrate! She grabbed Winona by both hands and began to dance with her up and down the dusty road adjacent to the property. It was a sight to behold! Here were two elderly ladies dancing energetically while young boys were playing their plastic bongo drums. Then, the police arrived!

The dancing stopped. The music stopped. Everything got very quiet. Haiti is one of the most violent nations on planet earth and the presence of police meant there was serious trouble. There were five cars loaded with armed policemen. They all moved out of their vehicles and glared at our leader, Maxo, and at the American missionaries. "What are you doing here?" the surly commander shouted in a loud voice. "What are you white people doing here?" he repeated in French. "Come and explain to them, Mamee!" Maxo called out to Mamee. Everyone felt the tension as 15 armed policemen looked at us as if we were criminals.

Little 85-year old-Mamee, weighing less than 90 pounds, came striding up the hillside carrying a document in her hand and waving it at the commander of the police. "I want you to know!" Little Mamee walked in front of each of the policemen waving her document. "I want you to know," she repeated in her high-pitched Creole voice. "I want you to know that I prayed six years for someone to come and build us a school and a church and now they are here. Here is the deed that gives them the right to build and you had better get out of here and leave them alone!" There was dead silence as the chief of police read the document. Then, he looked at his squad of policemen and said, "I think we had better leave!"

What joy and celebration followed that crisis! We all breathed a sigh of relief as the work continued. But, Mamee had other plans. She walked briskly down to her little one-room house and returned in a few minutes wearing her only church dress. She came walking up to me, "Papa-san," and pointed that bony little finger at me and said, "We are going to have church right here and, you Pastor Jack, are going to preach!" Wow! I was astonished, but I was not about to deny that little Hero of the Faith. I could only answer in the affirmative, "Oui, Mamselle!"

There on that poverty-stricken mountainside in Pernier, Haiti, we experienced another miracle that day. It was even greater than the miracle of "chicken and rice." As I gave the message, followed by the invitation to receive Christ into our hearts, we were blessed beyond measure as almost every one of those men, women, boys and girls came forward to receive Christ as their Savior. I will never forget that day. Neither will Charlie Collins, our Haiti Overseer, or Adam Bryan, a young man who helped us start our work in Bolivia. But, most of all, I'm sure that Winona and little Mamee will forever remember the day when God blessed them with those beautiful miracles. I believe that one day these two saints will dance again up there on the streets of glory while heaven will clap its hands in Haitian rhythm.

2

Miracles in Santa Cruz, Bolivia

Winona and I had lived and worked in Bolivia during the mid-1950s. We had seen many miracles during those years we spent in La Paz and down in the tropical mountains of the North Yungas. While living there we were so blessed to be able to provide a home for a small group of young orphans. Three of those decided to follow the footsteps of Jesus and become ministers of the gospel. Their names were Bernabe and Agustin Luna, brothers, and Miguel Escobar, cousins to each other. All of them had moved to Santa Cruz, located in the southern part of Bolivia in the Amazon River Basin.

We had not seen our "orphans" for more than 40 years when we were privileged to travel to Santa Cruz in the mid-1990s. That short visit changed our lives, theirs and many other precious lives in that tropical city, now the largest in Bolivia.

What we did not know about these precious families was that they had worked and studied so hard for a number of years in order to do ministry to their countrymen. It was so thrilling to listen to their recounting of the degrees they had earned, the different jobs where they had worked and the struggles they had faced. They were overjoyed to "rediscover" Señora Winona and me since we were the only family that they had. They now had beautiful children, all of them highly trained and each one having a strong relationship with Christ. One of our greatest joys was to hear that they claimed us as their parents and grandparents since they had no other family.

It wasn't long after that Bernabe Luna and his wife Karina revealed to us that for years they had been praying and hoping for their own ministry in the Santa Cruz area. Bernabe and Karina were ordained ministers. Bernabe had attained college degrees and was a professor of art in a large evangelical school. Karina had her nursing degree and had worked for a number of years in that profession. Their older children were all working toward teaching degrees and the younger son and two daughters were about ready to graduate from a highly accredited evangelical school.

"Pastor Jack, we would love to share our dream-vision with you before you and Winona return to America," Karina shared with me the night before we were to leave for America the next morning. "Yes!" I answered as we walked out into their small patio, where we would share a vision that would change that section of Santa Cruz. For several minutes I listened with an open heart to these precious children who, more than 40 years before, had been orphans and had been so desperately poor. The last time Winona and I had seen the Luna and Escobar families their only possessions were faith, dreams and visions. Now the time had arrived for the fulfillment of years of faith, hope and dreams. I was so excited. I realized that we were standing on Miracle Territory.

Winona and I left for Miami and Indianapolis the following morning after dozens of hugs, kisses and words such as: "Te amo!" (I love you!) "Don't forget us!" "You are our grandparents!" "Please come back soon!"

Those words and embraces warmed our hearts as we flew across the Andes and on to America. We knew that we must return. We did not know how we could possibly afford to open a church or a school, but we knew that this was God's plan and He would provide. Our hearts and minds were filled with every type of question. The "enemy" tried to discourage us, but we felt in our hearts that this was a dream-vision in the making.

We had been involved with the Jamaican mission for more than seven years and were about to leap across the Caribbean to Haiti. It was then that we felt the compulsion to go back to Bolivia. We did not know exactly what we would do there, but we knew that we must go. Already, Pastor Bernabe, Karina and family had started church services in the *barrios,* the poorest neighborhoods of Santa Cruz. We received exciting e-mails telling us that they were holding worship services outdoors and that a lot of people were attending.

We heard an astounding account of one service where the rains started to fall and Pastor Bernabe tried to dismiss the fairly large attendance. He asked them to please hurry and find shelter from the now drenching rain. He could not believe what he saw and heard. "We want to hear the Word! We do not want to leave! Please continue with the message!" I could hardly keep back the tears as I read more and more of that special account. "Pastor Jack and Winona, they would not leave! It was now raining hard and they insisted on staying to hear the precious news that Jesus loved them, died for them, etc." Finally, according to Bernabe, he stopped the message and they all ran for cover. We were overjoyed to hear of such faith, love and willingness to suffer inconveniences in order to worship their newfound faith.

Winona and I were eager to go back to see our "adopted children and grandchildren" in their new roles as missionaries to their own people. We were hearing so many stories of how these new converts were eager to fast and pray for needs in their lives, their Bolivian neighbors and even us! It was an awesome revelation!

Then, to top it all off, we got the word from our Santa Cruz leaders telling us that the young Luna sons and one son-in-law had recruited an entire soccer league of young boys in the neighborhoods and they were coaching them, sharing the Word of God and praying with them on a biweekly basis. Already more than 150 young athletes were a part of our Christ Community Football League. I could hardly wait to see this.

As we prepared to go back to Santa Cruz, Bolivia, to see the miracles that were taking place, we had a telephone call that turned into a wonderful miracle. Our son, Stephen, called us a few months prior to tell us that one of his former students at Heritage Christian Academy, in Indianapolis, was asking about the possibility of going with us on a mission trip to Haiti. This young man, Adam Bryan, proved to be key to the success of the future of Bolivia. While in Haiti, Bryan had his heart touched by the poverty of the people, the love of the children and watching the miracles that happened on that trip.

Adam had heard that we were planning to go to Santa Cruz and he called to inquire about the possibility of taking a group of teenagers from his church, the Nora Christian Fellowship. We agreed that this would be wonderful and we all began making plans for that "journey of a lifetime!"

Our Bolivian families were so excited the day that Adam Bryan, Sam Wilson, Jen Mayes and Janet Williams, the youth mission leaders, stepped off the plane in Santa Cruz and into the arms and hearts of many children, teenagers and adults who had been waiting for that moment.

The next few days were filled with many types of ministries among the children and adults. The Nora Fellowship team worked very hard chopping down brush and weeds from a building site. Some members of the team helped plant bananas while others ministered to the young boys of the soccer league. But, the "real miracles" were still waiting in the wings.

"Tonight, we are showing the *Jesus* film out on the soccer field," we announced to the Nora team. It was not necessary to announce our arrival on that miracle night in the tropical Amazon Basin. The word spread like wildfire and soon the area was filling with children and adults, most of them sitting on the ground. We felt a concern for many of the small children who came to the service since they were only wearing thin garments and most were barefooted. Then, the cool winds began to blow and children and adults began to shiver.

I realized that the movie would last another hour or so and that the families might leave due to the brisk, damp winds. I remember whispering to Janet Williams, one of the youth escorts, "Let's pray that God will touch their hearts and they will come forward to receive Jesus." Janet agreed and passed the word along to other members of the team. Finally the beautiful story of Jesus ended. No one had left during the showing. I felt the Lord telling me to go to the front of the audience and invite them to come forward for salvation. We could hardly believe our eyes.

Almost everyone, young and old, came to the front of the basketball court, where many were seated. I asked them, "How many of you want to accept Jesus as your Savior?" Almost every hand was lifted. There were others who were already believers and these wanted special prayer for other needs. All of our hearts were filled with joy as we all prayed in unison the Sinner's Prayer and our declaration of faith. This was followed by hugs, smiles and expressions of joy. We then asked them to line up to receive New Testaments in the Spanish language. We had never seen such eagerness and excitement as the lines of people could hardly suppress their impatience to obtain their own copy of the Word of God.

We did not realize, that cold, windy evening, that other miracles were waiting in the wings.

Our pastors and leaders asked each convert if they would like to be baptized on Sunday, a couple of days later. We then hired three buses to take all of the candidates to a large pond-river located some 30 miles out in the tropical interior. There we saw more divine miracles happening among those beautiful new Christian brothers and sisters. One of the first happened with the busload of children.

The driver decided to take a different road to our baptismal site. All of the roads were narrow, winding and pure sand. Many times it was necessary to do some pushing to get through sand drifts in the road. The busload of children got stuck while crossing a river. The water was more than two feet deep and the bus got wedged in the deep sand and water. He had taken a different road thinking it would be easier to navigate. Now, he was stuck with more than 35 children and he had no way to communicate with the rest of us for assistance. What was he to do? After several attempts to drive through the water the driver decided that it was futile, but the children had a solution! They asked if they could get out of the bus, wade in the hip-deep water and lay their hands on the vehicle and pray. We could hardly believe the rest of the story!

The children, most of them under 12 years old, encircled the stranded bus and laid hands on it and began to pray in unison. Then, the driver pressed the accelerator and the large vehicle moved right out of the water. The children celebrated! God answered their prayers! A few minutes later this jubilant bunch of children joined us for the baptismal service. But, we had another problem! How could we solve this one? A teenaged young man from Nora Christian Fellowship taught us all a lesson of faith that day!

The wind had been blowing for more than two days and the sand was flying into people's faces, hair, mouths and eyes. It was irritating and slightly painful. Also, the sound of that strong south-pole wind made it difficult to be heard and we had come to this place to worship. "Why don't we ask God to stop the wind?" the teenage boy from Nora asked. I looked into the faces of those young American missionaries and saw the faith in their eyes that day. "Why not? Yes! Let's ask God to stop the wind so that we can have our baptismal and worship!" What excitement surged through those Nora Christian Fellowship teens and their escorts as we joined hands and began to pray in a symphony of praise and prayer, but nothing happened! We all looked at each other. "Let's get into the water!" I heard myself speaking.

All of those 19 American teenagers and their leaders waded out into the windy, sand-blown waters. Then, one by one, the new converts waded out to them to be baptized after Pastor Bernabe and I read the scriptures and heard the vows from the candidates. Then... it happened! The wind stopped! There was a heavenly silence. God stopped the wind! Our hearts were filled with praise. That was one of the most joyous baptismal services we had ever seen. Could anything be more wonderful than that? Yes!! And, it happened in the water without our knowledge! Listen to the rest of the story!

After that joyful day had ended following a delicious picnic and some praise and worship, we loaded up the three buses and headed back to Santa Cruz. Everyone was exhausted from that wonderful day and some of us were ready for a little *siesta*. Little did we know about the other miracle that had happened in that baptismal celebration! I heard it the next day.

"Pastor Papa-san, this lady wishes to tell you a story!" I looked up to see Señora Karina, Bernabe's wife, standing beside a lady in her mid-fifties. I listened that day to a marvelous miracle story that had happened the previous day. "I was dying of cancer," the lady shared with us, "and I did not have long to live. The cancer specialists had no hope for me. I had been praying for a miracle and it happened yesterday. While the people were entering the water the Lord spoke to me and said, 'go into the water!'"

"I could hardly believe it," she continued. "So, I waded into the water and they baptized me again. I never felt so good. I knew that something wonderful had happened so this morning, Monday, I went to the clinic and the cancer specialist did some testing on me. When he was finished he told me that 'your cancer is gone! You are free from all traces of cancer!'" We all celebrated again as we rejoiced in our Heavenly Father who still does miracles today!

As a sequel to this story we were so blessed when the visitors from Nora Christian Fellowship took pictures of the many boys and girls who needed a school. Within a few weeks from the time they left for the USA we were able to open the first Bolivian Christ Community School. We now have kindergarten through 8th grade and each day over 130 children hear about Jesus, then they stand together to sing and pray. On Fridays, before they leave campus, they all stand and point their hands toward the Wall of Prayer, where many of your names are written. They pray for you and us. They give thanks to El Señor Jesus for their school and for all of us. This is one of the most beautiful spectacles we have seen.

Will you pray today for these precious people in the Santa Cruz department of Bolivia? Recently a hostile army surrounded this city and it appeared that many of our people would be killed. This communist government wants to close down all Christian schools and churches in this area. We need a special miracle of protection for these children and their families.

3

The Miracle in Guy's Hill
in Jamaica

We have a fine school in Guy's Hill, a town located not too far from the capital city of Kingston, Jamaica. It is called Guy's Hill Basic School and is sponsored by Stone's Hill Community Church in Ligonier, Indiana. One day we received a call from Miss Althea Williams, the teacher-cook in the school. Althea is the daughter of Pastors Roysten and Cynthia Williams, the pastors and directors of our CCCWM church and Basic School. The call from Althea was urgent. "Pastor Jack, there is a 7-year-old boy here in this community and he has never been to school before. His mother came to see us and asked if we would consider allowing him to enroll in our school."

"Pastor Jack," Althea continued, "this little boy's name is Jayleen and he has never walked in his life. No school will take him and he really wants to be with the other children." I did not hesitate to tell Miss Althea that they should enroll little Jayleen if the teachers would be willing to carry him to the bathroom and other locations as well as loving and praying for him each day. The teachers heartily agreed.

The next visit we made to the school we were able to meet Jayleen. He was seated in a chair and was absorbed in his assignments. His little face was covered with smiles as he interacted with his teachers and other students. He was such a delightful child and he was having the time of his life. All of the teachers and other students loved Jayleen because he was so joyful. This was the fulfillment of his lifelong dream. Later we received another phone call from this same school and teacher, Althea.

"Pastor Jack, another mother called us and she wants to know if we will allow her little girl to enroll in our school? She has never spoken in her entire life but she is lonely and wishes to be with the children at the school." Of course, we agreed that this new little girl named Alexia should be allowed to enroll in our school. Within a few weeks we were able to meet this beautiful little girl named Alexia. Her face was covered with smiles. She communicated through hand signals. We enjoyed watching her color pictures and other simple assignments that required no vocal skills. She loved hugs and pats on the head. Winona and I were so pleased that we had been a small part in rescuing Jayleen and Alexia from their lonely world and introducing them to this vibrant, joyful student body in Guy's Hill, Jamaica. We had no idea that God was about to do two great miracles with these handicapped children.

We had heard by telephone that Jayleen and Alexia had experienced some wonderful answers to prayer, but we had no idea of the magnitude until we went to their graduation exercises in mid-June. We were overwhelmed and overjoyed by what we saw and heard that day. The entire graduating class stood proudly in front of the church that was filled with families and friends. The class sang some special songs of worship and praise. One of the voices rang out louder than the others. Could this be true? It was Alexia and she was singing at the top of her voice. Everyone in the audience realized that a miracle had happened to the child and they were celebrating with her. Then, it was time for the diplomas and awards to be given. Each child received his or her diploma and then walked out into the audience to show their parents and families. They called Jayleen's name! He stood up and walked to the rostrum to receive his award. Then... little Jayleen, who had been crippled since birth, was not just walking, he was running to the back of the church, where his family was seated. What a time of rejoicing and applause filled that little sanctuary that day.

Winona and I were filled with joy as we listened to Alexia saying to Winona: "Mama-san, please come with me and I will show you the pictures I have drawn! Mama-san, do you want to hear me count! One! Two! Three! Four!" Alexia could not stop telling about all the things she had done in school for the past weeks since God restored her voice. Little Jayleen could not sit down! He had been an invalid for seven years and now he could walk, run, skip and dance!

As we drove back towards Golden Grove, Jamaica, where Mama-san and I lived in a little concrete house perched on the side of a tropical mountain, we could not describe the joy we felt. Here were two precious miracle children who had been set free from their incurable handicaps through faith and prayer, of course! But...another factor was the love, kindness, patience and prayers shown each day by teachers and children who believe in a God of Miracles. They might have been some of the poorest children in Jamaica, but in my opinion they are some of the richest! They have Jesus as their friend.

4

The Miracle in the
Tucson Hospital

About three years ago Winona and I made a visit to our daughter, Melissa Fischer, and her husband Gary while they were still living in Tucson, Arizona. We had looked forward to a few days rest out in that beautiful desert environment. We had planned to walk each day with the puppies out in a cactus park located quite close to the Fischer home. We had been there before and had a delightful time riding across the beautiful landscapes in Missy's Jeep. Tucson, Arizona, in my opinion, is a vacationer's paradise. I had no idea that I was about to undergo a serious physical emergency.

Then the heart attack hit me like a lightening bolt. The pain was severe in my chest and made breathing difficult. I prayed about it and delayed telling the family as long as I could. The pain became more intense and I found myself thinking that I might be in serious jeopardy if I did not disclose some of the symptoms to Melissa, who was the Director of Surgery at St. Joseph's Hospital in Tucson.

A lot of thoughts raced through my mind on that bright Saturday morning as Missy drove me to see one of the top heart specialists in that part of Arizona. As usual I questioned, "Why?" I had recently gone through a number of crisis situations as a missionary living in Jamaica. There had been other surgeries. On one occasion I lost most of my vision and I had to make an emergency trip to Indiana to see a specialist. The eye specialists in both Jamaica and Indiana had diagnosed aneurysms and other major complications. But, minutes after preaching at Mrs. Mary Martz's funeral at Christ Community Church and sitting down in the front pew, I felt compelled to look up to where a beautiful cross was hanging. I had not been able to see my Bible that day. I had been unable to drive or do much of anything.

16

Everything was a misty haze. But, as I looked in the direction of the cross my eyesight was restored. I thought about that day as I waited to see the heart surgeon in Tucson.

I thought also of the time I made another trip to Indiana from Jamaica and I was carrying a heavy pain in my lower abdomen. I had endured that pain for several days before Winona and I came back to Indiana for one of our furloughs. When I went to see Dr. Erb for a check-up he immediately put me in the emergency ward at Riverview Hospital. Not only did I have a gall bladder that was severely infected, but my body was full of deadly infection. Had I waited a few more days it could have been fatal. The surgery went well and I was soon able to resume ministry. I thought about those two occasions, and others, as I awaited the examination and prognosis of the heart specialist at St. Joseph's Hospital. As usual I found it best to pray and thank the Lord for His goodness and mercy. I had so much to be thankful for. Winona and I had seen so many miracles in our lives. We knew that day that He could work another one. The diagnosis was very negative.

"You will need surgery, Mr. Terry," the specialist reported after viewing the many x-rays and other high-tech photos. In his Middle Eastern accent he tried to show us the large sac of water that had accumulated around my heart. I listened with a sense of dread as he outlined the need for me to be placed on the emergency surgery list for early Monday morning. I would have to stay in the intensive care ward with oxygen. I would not be able to get out of bed even to go to the bathroom. I heard this with the sense that I was facing a major battle and I would need lots of prayer.

This was Saturday and the day went slowly. I prayed as much as I could between the times of examinations, blood tests and other medical probes by the technicians and nurses. As night approached the surgery nurses gave me some sleeping medications. Soon, I fell asleep for a few hours and awakened in the early morning hours, around 2:30 a.m., with a powerful sense of God's presence in that intensive care room. I could not believe the joyful message that I heard in my spirit from my Heavenly Father.

"Get up and go to the window and pray!" I could scarcely believe what I was hearing in my spirit. "Take the oxygen tubes out of your nose and go to the window and pray!" Can this be for real? I am in intensive care! My daughter is the coordinator of surgery of this hospital and I have been diagnosed with a severe heart malady. My surgery is only one day from now! What must I do?

I knew that precious voice. That was my Great Shepherd and I knew His voice. He had led me through hundreds of crises, persecutions, and painful ordeals, as well as an untold number of miracles. I got up out of bed dressed in my skimpy nightgown that covered very little of my torso. I got up from that bed, took out the oxygen tubes and went to the window to pray. I never felt better. I knew that I had been healed.

It wasn't long until the attendants discovered that I had broken several of their stringent rules. I heard several mini-sermons, I think, about getting out of bed without assistance of a nurse or technician; about removing life-giving oxygen without a written order by the specialist; and much more. What will Winona say? What will Missy say? What did the Lord say? He said, "Get up! Get out of bed! Take out the oxygen tubes! Go to the window and worship!" Wow! That is what I had done and it was glorious.

I was forced to stay in bed during the rest of the day. I broke the rules as often as I could. Over and over during the day I would explain to three shifts of nurses and attendants that I was well. They all knew that I was a missionary and a minister. I got some strange looks during the day and a few, I think, rather quizzical remarks. At least the Heart Surgery Ward was aware that something strange was happening.

Finally, the heart specialist from the Middle East entered into my room. He had many questions. It was close to the scheduled time for my Monday morning surgery and it was still on the docket. After I explained that I would not need surgery he insisted that I should be taken, in a wheelchair of course, to the high-tech examination room where he would show me again that my heart was defective and I would need surgery to stay alive. My heart was full of joy and praise because I knew more than the top heart specialist in that region. I had heard from the Great Physician who lived inside my heart. He had told me that I was OK and I would never doubt that.

The examinations began. The x-rays and other photos were soon displayed on a large screen overhead. The well known heart specialist began to study the pictures of my heart and after a few minutes he looked at me and said, in that Middle Eastern accent: "I can't believe it! I can't believe it!" He said that over and over again. Then, the sweetest words I had ever heard him speak, "You do not need heart surgery. There is nothing wrong with your heart!"

Soon, the word spread! Soon, Winona and Missy were in my room. Soon, I was eating a hearty breakfast and getting packed to go home to Missy's house. Today is Monday! I can take my puppies, Natchez and Chaco, and we will go for a long walk in the desert park here in Tucson, Arizona. We will pray! Sing! We will rejoice! I will probably dance a little. Why? Because I have the greatest Heart Specialist in the Universe! And, so do you! Thank you Jesus, our Great Physician!

5

The Miracle of Jacob Bush and the Hurricane

The year was 1998 and I had just moved to Jamaica. I had decided to go to the Caribbean a few weeks ahead of Winona so that I could prepare the mission house for her arrival. I had already faced a number of trials, such as convincing a family of ten people to vacate the upstairs of that small concrete hurricane-proof dwelling that we had built for Winona and me. Fortunately, I was able to find them another place to live not far from the mission compound. Later we were able to help them build a small home on church property. Each day was a new challenge as I struggled to learn the culture, the *patois* language of the area plus the never-ending governmental requirements for permits, visas and registrations. I missed Winona. I spent as much time as possible praying and trying to get acquainted with the African descendants of slavery and centuries of abuse and maltreatment. Some of the children of the area were fearful that our coming to their neighborhood meant another regime of slavery. Several of the local Rastafarians, natives who worshipped the former emperor of Ethiopia, resented the presence of white Christian missionaries!

I had spent nearly one month in this beautiful, tropical mountainside community when I heard a startling weather report on my shortwave radio. A powerful hurricane was bearing down on the island of Jamaica and it threatened to destroy much of Jamaica. I was shocked by this announcement and was ill prepared to cope with the predicted devastation. I had heard many horror stories of previous storms that destroyed homes, blocked roads, ripped up the trees and vegetation and blew down telephone and electric wires. At this time I was dwelling in the upstairs of the fairly new mission house and there was no furniture, refrigerator, stove, running water or other modern conveniences. My furniture consisted of one air mattress bed and a small crock pot that allowed me to brew hot water for instant coffee. And, now a hurricane was heading our way and we were directly in its path. I began to pray fervently that the Lord would protect me and all of the poverty stricken people across the island who lived in tiny shacks in the interior and in the city ghettos.

I tried to concentrate on my assignments as a missionary to open schools and churches, purchase a van, and obtain permits and countless documents. But, most of all I prayed as the powerful hurricane approached (the Arawak Indian meaning of hurricane is "god of anger"). Questions flooded my mind, such as, What if this enormous and furious storm destroys our new Basic School which served, also, as a Sunday school and a church? What if the mission house that served as the missionary's home and also as a small orphanage should be blown away? The "enemy" tried to discourage me in many different ways, but we prayed and there were a lot of people praying in the USA. One of those "Prayer Warriors" was Jacob Bush.

Jacob Bush, the 5-year-old son of Jim and Karen Bush, lived a short distance from the Christ Community Church in Lamong, Indiana, where we had served as ministers for a number of years. Jacob was my friend and we enjoyed playing little games together. One of them was called, "I saw you first!" It was silly, but it was a lot of fun. Jacob prayed for us. It was a very special day when he saw on the TV news that Jamaica was about to be hit by a major hurricane. Jacob decided to do something about it.

That was a Miracle Moment when Jacob Bush brought his prayer request to the preschool classroom the next day. Jacob was very intense as he said to his teacher and mother, Karen Bush, "Pastor Jack is in a lot of trouble down in Jamaica. A hurricane is going to hit and he could get hurt! We need to pray for Pastor Jack!" The entire class of preschoolers got down on their knees to pray for Pastor Jack and Jamaica.

The meteorologists watching the storm edging toward Jamaica could not believe what they saw on their radar screens. Never, according to the experts, had they seen a major hurricane stop and turn the opposite direction. This one did! This hurricane named Mitch was moved miraculously away from Jamaica and the island was saved from destruction and devastation.

In Jamaica we celebrated this wonderful miracle and we gave God the praise. We knew that it was Him who had spared us, but we did not know the Jacob Bush story until later.

The next morning at the Christ Community Church preschool the children entered the classroom with spirit of celebration and praise. As the hurricane miracle was told and everyone had applauded, little Jacob Bush stood up with the rest of those "mighty little prayer warriors" and said, "See!"

Some time after the Hurricane Miracle, our precious Jacob suffered a devastating accident on a four-wheeled ATV that nearly took his life on May 12, 2001. Here is an account of that fateful day by Terry Moore, Jacob's (Jake's) close friend and mentor:

> I didn't learn of the events that occurred on May 12th until the following day, which was Sunday. It also happened on Mother's Day. My aunt had been watching the news and saw that "Jake" had been involved in a serious accident and had been life-lined to Methodist Hospital. My mother was able to patch through to the critical care unit. She relayed the information to me. Jake had been involved in an accident. He and his older brother had been riding the neighbor's four-wheeler when it flipped over. His brother was fine but Jake had suffered severe head trauma. He had also lost a great deal of blood, which caused him to have two strokes on the way to the hospital. The swelling in his brain had become so bad that the doctors were going to remove half of his skull to relieve the pressure
>
> The picture was so bleak. All that I could do was to pray for my little friend. I began to fast and pray. The surgeries and treatments continued for weeks. The doctors began to acknowledge the fact that Jake might survive, but that he would probably be in a coma for the rest of his life. We would not accept that theory. We kept praying. Karen, his mother, refused to leave the hospital. We just kept praying and hoping. His family and a lot of other people were praying also. Then, one day it happened!

Jake was now sharing a room with another little boy who was completely paralyzed. I had just told Karen that she needed to trust the fact when it was God's time things would work out, when inexplicably the light above the bed of Jake's roommate came on. As soon as the light came on, Jake opened his eyes wider than he had ever done before. He also picked up his right hand and leaned forward as if he was trying to talk. Karen and I were in shock. We both stood there with tears running down our cheeks. This went on for about an hour and then Jake went back to sleep after the light went out. We had seen a miracle.

As the days and weeks went by, Jake continued to improve very slowly. He was now receiving therapy twice a day and beginning to respond to verbal commands. By the time of his release from the hospital he could look around and move all four limbs. It was obvious that he understood what he was being told. Soon he began to make noises through his trachea and smile at certain things. Soon those noises became words and the words became sentences. That is when one of the most amazing things happened. He described in detail everything that happened in the accident.

Jacob told us about the four-wheeler that had landed on top of him. He recalled that he and his brother Joe were driving the vehicle, also. Then, Jacob paused for a second and said, "There were three angels also!" We were stunned and asked him the same question several more times to see if he would change the answer. He didn't! We asked what the angels were doing and he said that they just stayed with him. Then he told us there were two firemen who stood over the top of him and that they put something on his face. Jake went on to tell us that he went to the hospital in a helicopter. Jacob's father couldn't believe how detailed a description that he had given. Jake even told us that he had lost his shoes and that he had been taken to his house and that his dad came out and held him. And, there is more to the story!

When, Jacob regained consciousness following the accident he told his mother, Karen, these awesome accounts of his journey through space. These are the words of a 9-year-old child: "We were on our way to heaven. It was me, Jesus and God and when we got halfway there Jesus bent down and looked me in the eyes. 'I can't take you home now because you need to go back to your earthly home because you have things to do down there, but you will come to me one day!'" Jacob shared another celestial moment as he described what happened immediately following the accident when a heavy four-wheeler rose in the air and fell on his chest and body. He said, "I saw three guardian angels when I fell and God told me: 'God is love!'"

Jacob Bush is now 16 years old and is still crippled from that ATV accident. He cannot walk or run like other children his age, but he can still smile and I am sure that he still prays for his family and many of us. I know that one day when we all get to heaven we will see the angels applauding this precious young hero of the faith. I am sure that we will hear Jesus say: "Welcome Home, Jake!" Then, all of us will shout and dance with joy upon the golden streets of Heaven!

6

"I Just Found a Stack of Money!"

We have a growing number of schools and churches around the world. We are blessed to have so many selfless, giving teachers, pastors and other leaders. It is so amazing to compare the incomes of teachers in the Third World countries with those in America. The average teacher in Bolivia makes slightly over $100 per month and that has accelerated recently, due to the communist government that has elevated prices substantially. Our pastors in Bolivia serve as teachers and pastors.

The average teacher in Jamaica receives about that same salary or slightly less per month. But, in Haiti and India our dedicated teachers make less than $50.00 monthly. The average American teacher now earns more than that each day. In spite of these low salaries there have been times when the payrolls were hard to meet. Here is one of those "Miracle Money Moments!"

It was the end of the month in Jamaica and time to prepare the pay envelopes for all of our teachers and pastors who served so selflessly in places like Windsor, Silver Grove, Cornerstone Christian Academy, Guy's Hill and Waterloo. Winona and I had just returned from the *cambio* (money exchange) in St. Ann's Bay and were preparing to fill the pay envelopes for the different schools and churches across the island. The exchange rate that day was around 60 to 1, which meant that sixty Jamaican dollars was worth only one American dollar.

This was always a joyful time of the month because our teachers and pastors get paid only once per month and it was now close to "payday." Payday meant that they would have a little money for the bare necessities of life. It also meant that they could live another month and there might be a few Jamaican dollars left over for a bottle of Ting, their favorite island soft drink. Or, they might be able to buy a few of those delicious, hot Jamaican Patties. We could hardly wait to place the receipts plus the currency in their envelopes and take them to the different schools across the island. Then, we encountered a terrible, painful ordeal! I had filled about half of the envelopes and the money ran out. We were shocked! We looked, but the stacks of bills that we had brought from the *cambio* were all gone. Our hearts were full of pain. I began to weep and pray. I reminded our Precious Father of the pain and sadness this would bring to our precious, hardworking teachers and pastors. They would have no money for transportation, food and other expenses. I could only sit there and pray. We desperately needed a miracle that day. It seemed that we just sat, prayed, wept and waited. It would not be fair to give to one half of the teachers and pastors. But, what could we do? All of the funds that came from America had been converted to Jamaican money. Then it happened! I heard Winona scream! "Jack! Come here! Come and see!" I raced into the little bedroom where Winona had been sitting and writing out receipts and putting names on envelopes.

"Look! Look, Jack!" Winona was holding up a large stack of money. "I saw it on that shelf," she explained. "It was not there before," she exulted. Hallelujah! We could only clap, dance, celebrate and rejoice! How could this be? How precious, our wonderful Heavenly Father who can turn water into wine; He can multiple the fishes and loaves; and, He can multiply the Jamaican dollars! I believe that heaven celebrated with us that day. I began to fill the rest of the empty envelopes with a heart that was full of song and praise. And, when I finished filling the last envelope the money was finished, also. Can you imagine the joy that was ours as we drove to Windsor, Guy's Hill, and Waterloo, plus Silver Grove and Cornerstone?

He has promised that He would never leave us nor forsake us! For the past 57 years of our marriage and ministries around the world we have experienced His love and miracles. Sometimes He allowed us to go through some "fiery furnaces and lion's dens" of tests and trials, but that taught us that He will always provide for His children. Will you praise Him today that you are on His special list and that He loves you and will care for you for "time and for eternity"? Jesus is the greatest financial officer in the universe. He has promised us: "Give, and it will be given to you. A good measure, pressed down, shaken together and running over, will be poured into your lap" (Luke 6:38).

7

The Miracle of Deadly Worms

In the late 1950s, Winona and I lived as missionaries in the beautiful tropical town of Coroico, which is located at the end of the Yungas Road, "the world's most dangerous road," according to *National Geographic* magazine. The town of Coroico in those days had a population of approximately 3,000 people, counting the outlying suburbs. This was the town that had seen a spiritual revival after the first months that we had arrived. This was the community where it had been too dangerous to open the doors of the church to the street because they had threatened to stone us.

In the first days of our ministry in Coroico, located in the region called Yungas, we encountered some stiff opposition by the followers of *yatiri,* the worshippers of demonic ancient gods that reached back to the pre-Inca days. This religion had merged with the Catholic Church during the reign of the Jesuits, a radical group of zealots who believed that if the followers of a *yatiri* attended mass and took communion that they were Christians in spite of their demonic practices.

God provided a series of miracles for us there, such as raising a baby from the dead, the conversions of several young zealots that had entered the church to stone us, and enabling us to open a free clinic that supplied medications for the entire village as a result of a "miracle" visit by the head of the United Nations Medical Team. The surgeon-director of that UN team had come to our tiny clinic and agreed to provide, free of charge, all of the antibiotics and tuberculosis treatments that we could use.

Following those days, we saw the little mission move from a handful of elderly believers who had suffered many forms of persecution to a church that began to grow with a large group of believers, young and old. In fact, there were so many young people attending the services that we had to ask them to worship on Saturday nights to provide space for the rest of the growing congregation on Sundays.

Several different forms of ministry began to take hold in the community. The public-parochial school system invited me to be a teacher in the town of Coroico. This was unheard of previously in Bolivia. To our knowledge we were the only evangelical pastors that had ever been approved by the Archbishop of the Catholic Church in that South American country. This proved to be a great open door for the spreading of the gospel.

Other forms of ministry began to unfold in that new frontier for the gospel. The city officials asked me to become the coroner of the entire region. I had never had experience in those areas, but I was willing to learn and I did own a typewriter and now they could present a well written document to the higher officials in La Paz when someone died.

One of the most fruitful new ministries was in the area of athletics. Now that we had been accepted by the community we had an open door to work with the young men of the area. We were able to open volleyball and basketball leagues in addition to sponsoring a soccer team that participated in the entire region of surrounding communities. Our team chose the name, *El Strongest!* That was an admixture of English and Spanish since everyone was also eager to learn English and many were coming to the mission to take classes. But, medicine proved to be the most effective open door next to the preaching and teaching of the gospel. Here is one of those "miracles."

People came to the clinic for all sorts of treatments. Sometimes I was baffled as to what to prescribe. For example, there were kids who would put coffee beans in their noses for fun and then couldn't get them out. The main reason was that the bean would swell and in a short time would extend roots that would enter the tissue of their noses. My only solution was to do surgery with tweezers. I would cover the area and tweezers with antiseptic and then begin probing by flashlight into the dark interiors of little twitching, squirming noses. After grasping the swollen bean there was only one way to extract the coffee bean and that was to yank it out as quickly as possible. This was always accompanied by loud squeals and shrieks, but it worked and in a few moments after the blood was staunched the little coffee bean victims would begin to smile and ask if they might keep the bean as a souvenir. But, there were other forms of sicknesses and diseases in the community that were deadly. Tuberculosis was the main killer, but now we were able to help curb much of the epidemic through mass injections of a special medication provided by the UN Medical Team. Another malady in our community was *worms!*

I saw this young child while I was walking down a dirt road that led out into the agricultural areas where vegetables and fruit were grown. Also, some of the largest fields of cocaine in the world were found in this area of Bolivia. Many of the older generations had chewed the leaves to relieve hunger and pain. This was one of the main reasons that the typical male only lived to the age of 38 to 40 years. Intestinal worms were another killer! This little boy was walking down the road in the same direction that I was going. I noticed that his stomach was protruding severely and he seemed to be listless and weak. "What is wrong with your tummy?" I asked the 7- or 8-year-old child as we walked in the shade of the beautiful palm trees and listened to the squawking of colorful parrots. "Yo tengo gusanos!" the little boy answered as he looked at me with those sad, brown eyes. "I have worms," he explained. "Y, voy a morir," the precious little child explained. "I am going to die!"

I knew that we must do something immediately for that innocent little boy. As usual I would pray and ask the Lord to show me what to do. I had received only a basic training as a blood technician with the Arkansas State Board of Health and as an X-ray technician with the Indiana State Board of Health. I knew nothing about deadly worms.

"Where is your mother?" I asked the little boy. We just happened to be on the same road where the child and his family lived in an adobe hut thatched with palm leaves. Soon we arrived at the tiny house and the mother met us at the door. I asked her the same questions that I had asked her son and she confirmed that his life was in jeopardy. "May I take your son to our clinic?" I asked the mother. "I believe that we have some medicine that will help him," I explained.

"Oh! Yes Señor! Please help us! Our son will die of this sickness," she explained. Within a few minutes the little boy and I were climbing up the gentle slope that led to Coroico, where our mission church and small clinic were located. I looked on the shelf and found the medicine that I had remembered. The name of this special prescription was Vermifuge, and the label indicated that it was for intestinal infections and bacteria. I gave the little boy with the swollen tummy the entire contents of the bottle. I realized that we were facing a deadly enemy.

Within a few hours a transformation took place. The little boy began to emit long worms from several openings in his body. Some worms were evacuated from his bowels while others were vomited from his mouth. The final dead-worm count was more than 100 parasitic invaders. Within a few days the little boy was completely well. But, where was the miracle?

The following Sunday I was standing in the pulpit giving the message when I noticed a family entering the church from the street that ran alongside our chapel. I looked closely and I could not believe my eyes. There stood the little boy that had been delivered from an army of worms and he was holding his mother by the hand. His brothers and sisters were with him, and also, his daddy! They were smiling as they entered the church for the first time. Their son had been dying and now he was alive and well! They were thankful. That morning as I finished my sermon I gave the invitation for people to come to the altar and be saved. As we sang the invitation hymn that day we witnessed one of the most beautiful scenes on planet earth. The little boy and his entire family came forward to receive Jesus as Lord and Savior. That was the miracle!

I hope that all of you will get to meet that precious family one day in heaven. But, I want all of us to meet that unknown person who gave the few dollars to buy that prescription. That was not part of the United Nations medications. Jesus knows who did it and one day it will be celebrated up there just as it was that day in the tropical mountains of Coroico when "angels rejoiced in heaven" as an entire family was made whole!

Do you remember the little boy who shared his lunch of fishes and loaves with Jesus up in Galilee? Jesus can take your love gift of any size and use it to bless the hungry, the poor and the sick. Thank you for giving to the Lord!

8

"They Came to Kill You Last Night!"

Her name is Rosie Hanson and she lives in Golden Grove, just across the valley from the Mission Compound that provides two schools, a church, a mission house, a small orphanage, and three houses for the homeless plus 8 acres of beautiful tropical land. On this property we also have a basketball court, a children's playground, a bamboo prayer hut, and a 4,000-gallon water reservoir provided by the CBN television network. Also, you will find many beautiful banana, coconut, papaya and other Jamaican fruits. Some of my favorite parts of the mountain are located on the trails that have been opened by machetes and plastic prayer chairs stationed in more than sacred locations. For a number of years we had a prayer-treehouse on the very top of the mountain and people could climb there to pray, meditate and also see some of the most beautiful scenery in the Caribbean.

Rosie Hanson is the wife of D.J. (Disc Jockey) Hanson, who was named that after he recorded a number of CDs. Rosie is a fine Christian wife and mother of four children. I was honored to do her wedding shortly after we moved to Jamaica in 1992. Rosie and family are special friends.

One morning I answered a knock at my door and it was Rosie Hanson. Winona was absent from Jamaica at that time with the young crippled teenager named Jannel Hamilton. That is a miracle story in our first book. She was very excited and could hardly wait to come inside and disclose her secret. She spoke rapidly in her *patois* language and I was absolutely overwhelmed by her disclosures. "They came to kill you last night, Pastor Jack!" Then she told me the details.

"Last night, fairly late, we saw a man drive up into the small park-

33

ing lot across the road from the church. I and my young daughter had been sitting in the dark at the bottom of the hill just outside the church. The man looked up at your house and then checked to see if anyone was on the compound. Then he put a gun in his belt. He then began to walk up the 42 steps to your house!" Rosie continued with her story. "My daughter and I knew that you were in serious danger so we started to pray for you. I told my little girl to walk quietly to the other side of the church and go up the other set of steps and knock gently on Kevin Coulson's door. I sent word for him to pray for Pastor Jack also."

Sister Rosie, as we call her, looked at me and I could detect traces of tears in her eyes as she told me this miracle story. "Pastor Jack, the man came to your door and he pulled out his gun and then reached with his other hand to knock on your door. We knew that he was going to shoot you when you answered the door. Pastor Jack we were praying with all of our hearts! And this is what happened!" Sister Hanson paused to catch her breathe and then continued with this miracle story.

"Pastor Jack, we could not believe what we saw! The man stood there with his gun aimed at the door and his other hand ready to knock. He couldn't knock! He kept trying but something stopped him! He stood there for a long time and, then, finally in disgust he put his gun in his waist band and walked down to his car and drove away! We all celebrated because we knew that angels guarded you last night and stopped that killer from knocking at your door!"

Needless to say Rosie and I celebrated with joy and thanksgiving. We praised and thanked our Heavenly Father who had heard the prayers of those precious Jamaican believers and stopped the killer that dark night on the side of a mountain in Jamaica. I will never forget that story! I owe my life to Rosie Hanson who lives on the other side of the mountain in a tiny little hut with no modern conveniences. She might appear to live in poverty by American standards, but Rosie is wealthy beyond compare. She is a daughter of the King of Kings and He hears her voice. Thank you, Rosie! Because you also prayed for me that night and the angel of protection answered your prayer!

9

The Miracle of Hurricane Ivan and the Prayer Chairs

The hurricane had roared and raged most of the night. We had seen a miracle earlier in the night as the team members from Church of Praise, near Westfield, Indiana, had prayed and claimed victory over the storm. The meteorologist had predicted a devastating storm across the island of Jamaica. And, the first winds and rains were torrential and the winds had risen to nearly 100 miles per hour. But, during that "miracle evening" the storm subsided in Jamaica, turned abruptly to the west and moved into Cuba and Florida with destruction and havoc. We had been saved! Around 2:00 a.m. the entire team plus Winona and I decided to climb back up the hill to our little mission house for some badly needed rest. We were so joyful that the storm had calmed to moderate winds and rains. As we entered our house we discovered that a lot of water had dashed through the small openings under the roof and the grilled windows. We decided to ignore that for the evening and get some sleep. It was pitch dark inside the house and we all had to "feel" for the correct beds, rooms, etc. Soon everyone was asleep, but I needed to go to the restroom. I had no idea how dangerous that turned out to be.

I felt my way out of our bedroom, through the small living room and, finally found the tiny bathroom. I was happy for that successful venture, but I had no idea what was ahead. As I crept silently back to Winona's bedroom I discovered that I had made a very serious error. As I moved, barefoot, across the floor I felt the edge of a mattress on the floor. Oh! No! Then, in the silence of that dark dungeon I heard the unmistakable sound of several feminine snores. I was terrified! I was trapped! I did not know where the door was located and if I moved in any direction I might stumble and wake the ladies, all six

35

of them! Then, someone would scream and the entire work team of 12 people would attack me thinking I was a thief in the night! What was I to do? I prayed fervently and quietly! This was much more frightening than any hurricane! I asked for "guidance and direction" out of that room of prayer warriors that had just helped stop Hurricane Ivan. God heard my prayer and miraculously I found the one little door that had evaded me previously. Soon, I was in my own bed and I slept like an angel. The next day we saw another wonderful miracle.

The next morning we awoke to find that the storm had subsided to a drizzle and the wind was only a whisper. As we looked around the mountainside in Golden Grove we saw devastation all around us. Some trees had been uprooted while others had been stripped of their leaves. Electric wires were all down and there was debris everywhere. One special little survivor of the storm caught our attention. During the heavy hurricane winds a little bird had been seriously injured. When we picked it up it was trembling and its head kept drooping as if it had no strength at all. We held the little trembling, dying creature in our hands to warm it. Then, we realized that our Heavenly Father loves little birds, also, so we prayed that it would survive. When the prayer was finished the tiny little bird began to flutter its wings. I released it from my hands and it flew out the door and across the valley as if it had been totally revived. We celebrated with the little creature. All of the men in the group decided that we would try to climb the mountain where our schools, church, mission house and homes for the homeless are located. At the top of this mountain we had built a treehouse that provided a breathtaking view of our tropical surroundings. We all wanted to know if it had withstood the storm. This treehouse had been used as a prayer site for more than four years.

Several lovely trails had been chopped up the side of our eight-acre mountain compound. All of the trails were now blocked by uprooted trees, limbs and other debris. We had to chop our way slowly up the side of the mountain. We were moving at a snail's pace, but we were rejoicing in that we had heard of no injuries in our community or that anyone's home had been destroyed. Soon we came to the first of our prayer stations. We could not believe our eyes. Large trees were blown down in every direction, but our first prayer station was intact. Each prayer station consisted of a lightweight plastic chair weighing approximately 2 pounds. Also, these were chairs that had been broken or damaged in the Cornerstone Christian Academy and had been discarded. In most cases the chairs only had three legs and the fourth leg was supported by a rock. The chairs were very flimsy and could be toppled with the slightest touch. But, not this time!

These chairs had been the holy places where volumes of prayer, praise and intercession had been offered up to God throughout the previous months and years. Many spiritual battles had been fought in these different locations. This first chair was still standing in spite of winds that had exceeded 90 miles an hour? We all rejoiced and praised God for this miracle! But, was it just a freak accident that kept that one chair standing in the mighty storm? We now climbed and hacked more purposefully and joyfully. Could it be true? Our hearts were pounding as we climbed up the steep slope of the mountain that we had earlier named "Mt. Moriah"! Then we realized that we were standing on Holy Ground. We hacked our way from prayer chair to prayer chair. Not one had moved a centimeter. It was scientifically impossible! But, we realized that angels guarded those holy sites and no storm could blow them down.

One of our dear brothers was so blessed by what he had experienced that morning that he asked if he could sit in the last chair, number 8, I believe. All of us were now feeling the Spirit of praise and worship so we heartily agreed to pray over him, and to take our turns, also. I cannot explain what happened next. As our dear brother sat down in that sacred chair he was jolted by an invisible force and he fell to the ground. We realized that we needed to approach that chair with a greater sense of reverence and worship. We all prayed and were granted the peace and permission to sit, one by one, in that flimsy, cracked plastic chair while the entire team laid hands upon our heads and prayed for us. We all felt that we had been to a holy place that morning and we all knew that we would never forget that heavenly experience.

Many of you were also praying for Jamaica that night, and it was the combination of prayers that saved countless lives and properties. Prayer is the greatest gift that we can offer to God in behalf of those who are in the face of storms or other needs. Will you pray for the lost souls in America, Jamaica, Bolivia, Haiti, India and other places around the globe? It is the most powerful ministry that we know.

10

The Dead Baby Moved!

The mission team from Stone's Hill Community Church in Ligonier, Indiana, had just finished their work and worship projects in Jamaica and were preparing to return to Indiana the following day. Everything had gone well during the previous week and everyone seemed excited about the many people they had blessed in the churches and schools across the island. One of their projects was to plant banana trees in the mission garden located on the side of a tropical mountain.

Some of the ladies were preparing for sleep on the second floor of the Cornerstone Christian Academy building. Their dormitory consisted of air mattress laid on the concrete floors. Everyone had just finished their supper and was looking forward to a good night's rest. The ladies had selected the elementary classroom of the Academy building for their sleeping quarters. One of our American ladies was Daphne Long and she had made some wonderful contributions to the team's ministries. Daphne was more than six months pregnant and her husband had been reluctant for her to make this particular mission trip. Daphne felt that the Lord wanted her to come to Jamaica and all of us were convinced that she had been a great blessing to everyone. As Daphne was preparing her bedding for that night's sleep something tragic occurred! Daphne tripped and fell very hard on the cement floor. The impact of the fall was absorbed on her stomach and the pain was excruciating.

Daphne was stunned for a few minutes as she caught her breathe. Then, as the moments passed by, Daphne realized that something very serious had happened to her and the unborn baby.

For the past few weeks, Daphne reported, that the baby was very active within the womb. She could feel the baby's kicking and motions throughout the day. In fact it seldom was still for more than a few minutes at a time. Now, following the very hard fall the baby had not moved at all. Daphne waited patiently for some sign that the precious child was OK. The minutes passed by, but no movement. Now, Mrs. Daphne Long began to feel a very deep concern. This had not happened even once since the embryo had started its movements several weeks prior. Daphne began to pray. Then, some frightening questions began to enter her mind. What will my husband say if this turns out to be serious? Where can I find some medical care here in Jamaica? Would I have time to catch an emergency flight to America? What should I do? Daphne knocked at the mission house door.

I was deeply concerned as I listened to Daphne's account of the hard fall onto her abdomen on the cement classroom floor. I realized that we were facing a very serious dilemma and that we must do something very quickly. It was out of the question to try to escape Jamaica at that time of night since all international flights were closed until the following day. Also, to find expert medical treatment in our area would be almost impossible. We were faced with a very serious emergency and there was only one solution: Prayer! We must pray and trust our Great Physician for Mrs. Daphne Long and her precious unborn child.

I felt that we needed others to pray with us for our desperately needed miracle. We were so blessed to have Pastor Bucky Buckles, youth pastor from Stone's Hill Community Church, with us at that moment. Bucky and I began to pray for Daphne and her baby. We felt that we should walk with Daphne around the basketball court and pray in concert. So, we were determined to walk and pray through the night until we received an answer. Satan tried to discourage us to try other alternatives. We were resolute in our decision to walk and pray.

We walked, prayed, praised, worshipped and believed that our Father would not leave us nor forsake us. Ever so often we would check with our deeply troubled young expectant mother to see if the baby had moved. We walked and we walked. The minutes ticked by as we walked through the tropical night on that basketball court located on a hillside in Jamaica. There was no movement.

How many times we repeated our praise, our worship and our great request for this young mother. We were determined to walk until we got an answer. Nothing changed! Then…the most beautiful sound we could possibly imagine escaped from Daphne's lips. She screamed: "It moved! My baby moved! It's alive!"

That little Jamaican basketball court turned into an amphitheater of praise and worship. We were jubilant! We were dancing in our spirits! We checked Daphne's pulse and other vital signs and everything was normal. The baby seemed to be celebrating with us.

I will never forget that night when Our Jehovah Jireh (our Provider) showed mercy and grace and revived that unborn baby. It was difficult for us to finally settle down and try to get some sleep that evening because we had seen with our own eyes a "miracle of reviving a dying infant."

11

A Miracle Warning of "9-11"

We were having worship that night, September 10th, and the time was around 8:30 p.m. We were in the Golden Grove, Jamaica, Christ Community Church in a worship service. The singing, praying and testimonies had ended and the pastor, Winston Stewart, was about to begin the evening teaching session. Then…a tragic message entered my mind. I had heard this type of "voice" from heaven in the past and I knew that something horrible was about to happen. I sat there as the dark, dreadful details entered my mind and then throughout my entire body. What was I to do? The teaching had begun and would, most likely last more than one-half hour. I knew that I couldn't wait. I had to do something. I stood to my feet and asked that we stop the service. Everyone looked at me with astonishment.

I asked Pastor Stewart to give me the microphone for an urgent announcement and prayer request. This is what the Lord had revealed to me, an aged missionary living on a mountainside in the interior of Jamaica, West Indies. "God has spoken to my heart and told me that something terrible is about to happen to the United States and Jamaica," I shared with a troubled voice. "I believe that we must stop the service and all go to the altar and pray for America and Jamaica!" Soon, the entire church was on its knees at the altar and we were praying in symphony for the troubled request. After a few minutes of intercession the service was dismissed and we all went silently to our homes. I had a great deal of trouble sleeping. The ache was so heavy on my heart and mind. We had no way to confirm if anything had happened in America or Jamaica since there was no radio or TV on our compound.

The next day I spent much of the time climbing the hillsides and praying for that very strange prayer burden. I heard no news throughout the entire day. There were newspapers in the city of St. Ann's Bay, but no one had stopped to tell us what might have happened. Was it just my imagination? Was it an attack from the enemy with a false fear report? I continued to walk and pray. The burden would not go away. Then, I heard the voice of Mrs. Dawn Moses, wife of Pastor Phillip Moses, and her voice rang out across the mountainside. "Pastor Jack did you hear that there is a war in America?" I moved as quickly as possible to get the details. "There is a war in America and airplanes are crashing into buildings in New York," she exclaimed.

Within a few hours we had the full details of the terrorist attacks against the Twin Towers and other targets in America. As I listened I received a full confirmation that this was the fulfillment of the warning I had received the previous evening. Did other Christians receive that same message? I think so! I sincerely hope that they listened and began to pray. I will always believe that the attacks would have been much more destructive if we had not listened to the warnings and began to pray without ceasing for America and Jamaica.

Many will ask me, perhaps, "Why did the Lord mention that Jamaica would suffer, also?" Perhaps, very few will recollect that following the Twin Tower attacks the economy in Jamaica plummeted. The reason being that tourism, our primary source of income in the Caribbean, came to an abrupt halt following those attacks. Airlines were almost empty for many weeks following that incident. Hotels and other businesses suffered great losses. Many Jamaicans lost their jobs. It was a financial holocaust!

I will never forget that tragic moment in the history of America and Jamaica, but I will always be grateful to my Precious Heavenly Father who spoke to my heart that night in Golden Grove and gave all of us a warning. I believe that the prayers that ascended from the altars and from the mountainside where we have several prayer chairs made a significant difference in the amount of destruction in America during "9-11!"

Winona and I feel that, perhaps, other attacks are being planned by the terrorists of the world. Our only protection is prayer. Will you join us daily as we "stand in the gap" for America during this dangerous hour in history? Will you, also, recite II Chronicles 7:14 each day? It is a powerful prayer of protection!

12

Miracles in Israel

Israel is a miracle land! It is God's land and it has been given to the descendants of Abraham, Isaac and Jacob. Israel is now back in her own land after more than 2,000 years of exile, dispersion and persecution. It is very hard for most of us gentiles to even imagine the horrors of the Holocaust and other mistreatments of "The Children of Israel." The prophecy of Israel's return to her own land is one of the surest signs that we are living in the generation of Christ's return.

One of the greatest blessings for pilgrims to that sacred land is God's promise to Abraham: "I will bless those who bless you, and whoever curses you I will curse" (Genesis 12:3).

Winona and I have been so blessed to have been tour hosts to Israel many, many times. Here is an account of our last pilgrimage in December of 2006.

We had more than 35 "pilgrims" as we began our first day of journeys from Jerusalem to several sacred sites in Israel. For several months we had been praying and preparing for this "journey of a lifetime." It all began on November 1, 2006. We arrived in Tel Aviv on November 2nd and transferred to the Olive Tree Hotel in Jerusalem. We experienced so many wonderful memories: Bethlehem, Sea of Galilee, Nazareth, Caesarea, The Upper Room, The Garden of Gethsemane and the "Via Dolorosa."

In each of these places we sang, prayed, read the scriptures and took lots of pictures. At some sites, such as the Garden Tomb, we had the opportunity to take communion. Another wonderful moment was the "renewal of marriage vows" at Cana of Galilee, where each married couple recited sacred promises. But, one of the most holy sites for our group was the baptismal service in the Jordan River.

As we journeyed across the Holy Land our team of 36 people from a variety of denominations became "one in the Lord." We saw instances where those who had some animosity prior to the trip were totally reconciled. We saw others whose bodies had been suffering illnesses prior to the trip were now made whole. One of those was Eric Smith.

Brother Eric Smith had undergone several heart treatments, surgeries and other treatments. His condition had been so severe that he nearly had to cancel his trip. One day while our team was on the Mount of Beatitudes near the Sea of Galilee we laid hands on Eric and the Lord touched him in a mighty way. Eric was transformed from a hobbling, weak tourist into an energetic, almost running pilgrim. We were all so thrilled with that miracle.

We were blessed to have a minister from Las Cruces, New Mexico, join our team. He and his wife plus five other members from a Baptist church became "one in the Spirit" with our group. We felt that we had bonded for eternity. The pastor, Lyle Lionbarger, joined our group bearing a very heavy load of sadness and depression. He had suffered so many trials and tribulations prior to the trip to Israel and it was obvious that he was carrying a heavy cross. We laid hands upon Pastor Lyle at the Mount of Beatitudes, where Jesus did so many miracles, and our dear friend received a miracle of deliverance and joy. When Pastor Lyle gave the message at the open tomb, near to Golgotha, he was a transformed man and his radiant spirit was apparent to all.

One of our fellow travelers was Pastor Miguel Escobar from Bolivia. For many years Miguel had dreamed of making this trip. It had seemed impossible due to the expenses of traveling from Bolivia to America and then on to Israel. Miguel was so determined to make this holy pilgrimage that he borrowed money with the faith that he could pay it back in the near future. Miguel had a miracle trip, also, in that he experienced so many blessings at the holy sites plus receiving so much Bible knowledge. Miguel had been a very poor little orphan boy who had lived with Winona and me over 50 years ago. Now, Miguel is a pastor and a teacher in the Santa Cruz region of Bolivia. One of Miguel's greatest miracles happened after he returned to Indiana.

One of our fellow travelers spoke to me after the tour ended and asked about Miguel's finances. I explained how much it cost to travel from South America to Israel plus how different the salaries are in Miguel's area. Both Miguel and I were totally shocked and delighted when this same man said that he felt that he "should pay Miguel's entire travel expenses." What a time of rejoicing!

There were so many miracles that happened in Israel during this journey, but the greatest, perhaps, was the way our team bonded; the prayer meetings that were started to pray weekly for Israel; the spirit of joy that had infected each of us, and the financial miracles that happened in so many of our lives following the pilgrimage.

13

Jonathan Was a Martyr!

Jonathan Palomino was the 16-year-old son of Pastor Lorenzo Palomino, who was the local minister in the village of Coroico, Bolivia. During the 1940s and 1950s there was much religious persecution in that part of South America. Jonathan's father, Lorenzo, had been severely beaten on one occasion for his faith. He was taken to the local police station and beaten with whips because he would not give up preaching the gospel. I have heard that story a number of times and it always thrills me to know that when Winona and I, and our children, moved to that community the persecution miraculously stopped and the doors were wide open for evangelism in that district. The people told us that Pastor Lorenzo was beaten so severely that a Spanish guitar hanging on the wall resonated to the sound of the scourging. Lorenzo's mother begged her son to renounce his faith and give up preaching to avoid the scourging. Pastor Lorenzo's reply was, "Jesus died for me and I am willing to suffer for Him!"

When our family moved to that persecuted village in 1956 we were forced to endure opposition and threats for a period of time until God opened the doors and the entire community, it seemed, became our friends. But, in those first weeks we saw much opposition and maltreatment of our precious believers. One of them was our young hero named Jonathan, the pastor's son.

Jonathan was a high school student in that community and faced much persecution from the students, teachers and administration. Jonathan was whipped many times for his faith. Jonathan would never surrender his testimony and faith. He was a faithful witness in the church and community. We all loved Jonathan. The persecution and beatings took a heavy toll on this young hero of the faith. Jonathan became seriously ill. The best that we could determine was that he suffered from a serious heart ailment. Within a few days Jonathan died. We were totally convinced that he had been slowly murdered by the teachers, administrators and fellow students of his high school.

In that part of the world we had no funeral homes and we were obligated find a box for Jonathan's casket and bury him within 24 hours. It was the responsibility of the family to dig the grave. The next day after Jonathan's death we scheduled his funeral and burial at a gravesite that was dug on a beautiful Bolivian mountainside. This took place in July 1956. This was one of the most touching funerals that I ever conducted. A large number of young men attended this young martyr's funeral.

That day I was privileged to speak of this young hero and his faith. There were some great commitments made that day by those who attended. We wanted to sow more of the seed that Jonathan had planted. God answered our prayers and within a matter of months we witnessed many conversions among the young people of that area. Later I was asked to teach in the same school where my young hero suffered. Jonathan, in my opinion, was one of the great reasons that revivals came and persecutions stopped all across Bolivia. We will see young Jonathan one day at that great parade of "The Heroes of Faith" up in heaven. I can't wait my turn to run into his arms and thank him for his suffering and death that brought so many others to Christ. I love you, Jonathan!

We wholeheartedly believe that love is the most powerful weapon that we have to counteract the forces of persecution in today's world. Let's remember to love and pray for our enemies. St. Paul, the former terrorist against the early church, in I Corinthians 13:3 wrote: "If I give all I possess to the poor and surrender my body to the flames, but have not love, I gain nothing."

14

The Miracle of AIDS Healing in the Barrio

The following documentation of HIV-1 (AIDS) healing is one of the most powerful miracles we have seen. It is having a very positive effect on the people of this part of Santa Cruz who know about this miracle.

Michael and Daisy Lund are missionary founders of Vertical Life Ministries in Bolivia and they are working together with Christ Community Church World Mission in Santa Cruz. The victim in this miracle is Mrs. Olga Sosa Taboada and this interview was held after the medical confirmation of her miraculous healing.

> Michael: I apologize, Olga, if some of the questions I must ask will bring hurtful things to your remembrance. I thank you for agreeing to this interview so that others can see the entire picture of what God's grace has done in your life. So, with your permission, please tell me a bit about your experience with AIDS. What was life like for you and your family?
>
> Olga: I have one sister who lives here in Santa Cruz who was supportive. She could not help me financially but was always kind and never rejected us. Once we were officially put into the HIV Program, we had to identify ourselves to schools, hospitals, etc., whenever we wanted to use their services. Even though all four children tested negative for HIV, they were not allowed in any school. We were often not allowed to use the micros [small buses] if some of the people recognized us and complained to the driver. It was pretty much like that with everyone. I don't think they were bad people. They were just scared.
>
> Michael: How did you contract AIDS?
>
> Olga: Juan, my husband, contracted the disease over five years

50

ago and passed it on to me. He was depressed with no work and ashamed to be around his children because they were hungry. He did not often drink, but one night he did and went with another woman. When he came home that night he was so terribly depressed that he spoke of taking his life. I was intimate with him that morning to console him. Neither of us knew about the AIDS until a week later when he had symptoms. Juan secretly went to the doctor thinking that he had caught a common sexual disease. His blood test, however, revealed that he had contracted active HIV-1.

Daisy Lund: How were you told and what did you feel when you found you had also contracted the disease?

Olga: Juan came to me and confessed everything, saying that I must be tested immediately. I did, and the test came out positive. And from that day, I saw a fear come into my husband's face that I cannot describe…we were very concerned about this disease and feared for our children. And, so we immediately began to get information.

[Olga paused, emotional]

I know that you asked me how I felt when I was told and later when I found out that I also had the disease…. There is so much difference between you and me…that I don't know if I can make you understand…[another pause]. We were already poor. My husband was not lazy. He sometimes worked 10 or 12 hours just for a couple loaves of bread. We were poor, sister Daisy! We did not wake up in the mornings with any hope. We did not know if there would be work, any money, or bread that day…we lived with only one hope: that our children would not be poor, that they would study and somehow have enough luck in life not to be poor and without hope.

After finding out that we had HIV we woke up in the mornings wondering who would take care of our children when we died. That was the worst part…worrying what would happen to our children and knowing that they were going to go through the ordeal of losing both their parents, not only to death but to shame. For this, we felt like bad parents. And we felt that we must have done something terribly wrong that had cursed our lives.

Daisy: Was there no one in your husband's family here willing to take care of or help the children?

Olga: My sister promised to help but did not have enough even for herself. My husband's family rejected us. They were ashamed of Juan. And they were afraid. My mother-in-law would throw away anything the children touched in the house right in front of their eyes. My daughter is 13 and my oldest son is 11. They got their own information about the disease and asked us if there was any hope for us. There was none. Our children woke up every day wondering how much longer it would be until we died.

Michael: Did any of this make you think to turn to God for help? What was your relationship with God?

Olga: I believed in God but I was not a Christian. I did not want to be a hypocrite like my mother-in-law. I was poor but I was proud.

Michael: What did Juan tell the children before he died?

Olga: He asked them to forgive him for leaving them alone. He asked them not to blame me and not to blame God, just live good lives and be kind.

Daisy: How did you hear about Christ Community Missions Church?

Olga: Someone told me about this Mission School. They said that it cost nearly nothing. I was desperate. The children needed to be in school but no one would have them. So I went to talk to the lady [Karina Luna] who ran the school. I knew that the children did not have AIDS and so I made the decision not to tell the lady. Maybe I was wrong, but I was desperate. And I did not know what else to do.

Sister Karina and her family were very kind. They took the names and ages of my children and listed their names and arranged everything. The only thing that she asked of me was that I show an example to the children and come to the church service on Sunday night, February 4th, before the first day of school the next morning. I agreed. But I lived a long way away and was now eight months pregnant.

Daisy: But you ended up coming?

Olga: I left my other children at home with my oldest daughter. It was easier to travel with only Manuel and we arrived to the services a little late. Sister Karina and her daughter greeted me and took me to a chair. I felt uncomfortable. The place didn't really look like or feel like a church. But when the people started singing, I started to listen to the words.

They weren't singing words about God. They were singing *to* God. It felt strange. And I felt surprised. But then I was more surprised when I saw a *gringo* was the one who would preach. He preached about a man in the Bible, Naaman, who had an incurable disease and he started to compare the man's disease to AIDS. I was listening to the story and having no problem understanding now. And, what about me, I was thinking. "What am I supposed to do?" These thoughts were going through my head when all of a sudden, Brother Michael stopped preaching and came directly to me.

"I don't know you Señora," he said. "But do you know my Jesus? Have you asked Jesus to come into your heart and be your Lord and Savior?"

That night Sister Karina and Sister Daisy put their hands on me and prayed for me and my fear went away. Just like that, it went away. And in that same moment I knew God was about to do something I could not understand. I felt like time stopped. I prayed and asked Jesus to come into my heart. Sister Daisy and Karina continued to pray. They prayed for my baby. They prayed for my family and my life.

That night a miracle happened in the life of Señora Olga and her family. Here is the rest of the story.

Pastor Luis, one of our Christ Community pastors, took Sister Olga for a new blood test.

Olga: By this time I had disclosed to the leaders of Christ Community that I had AIDS. A week later the results came back and Pastor Luis called with this wonderful announcement: "It is negative, Olga! It's negative! You have won!"

Michael: What else would you like to tell us, Olga?

Olga: What can a person say? I want to thank everybody, but I know it was God who did this. I hope my husband is in heaven.

The church loved me enough to welcome me and not reject me even after they found out about the AIDS. My children are now in CCC Mission School. And the church has been helping us with money and food.

On July 11th, Winona, Steffani, our granddaughter, and I, Jack Terry, were so blessed to return to Bolivia where we were honored to meet Olga and her five children. We were greatly blessed to meet this precious hero of the faith. Here is the rest of her story:

I was so desperate to find a place for me and my children. I was eight months pregnant with my fifth child at that time. No one offered us a place to sleep or food to eat. The word was out that we were carriers of AIDS and we were treated as outcasts. We were not allowed to ride on public transportation. No school would accept my children. No church welcomed us until we found Christ Community. I was so desperate that I had planned to kill my children and then commit suicide to avoid further suffering and shame. Then…I met this church and school! Christ Community! I met Jesus! Now, I have a place to live, a place to worship, a school for my children, a place where people love us.

I will never forget that last evening we spent in Santa Cruz at a communion and farewell service planned for us. We received countless hugs, kisses and words of appreciation. Tears flowed freely that evening. Then, Olga stood up and came forward to stand beside me with her little family. She asked that a picture be made of all of us. Then, she made a little speech of appreciation and love. She handed two hand-woven jackets for me and Winona. They were beautiful. She now has employment in a large market place selling those hand-woven articles of clothing. I do not know the earthly value of our jackets, but I was moved to tears as I received mine. I will treasure it for the rest of my life. Señora Olga is one of my heroes. We will never cease to pray for this precious living miracle and her beautiful children.

15

A New Miracle in India

"Pastor Jack, I feel that you should come to India and open a school for the very poor children!" In 2006 I heard that powerful prophecy from Pastor Samantha-Naik, the India director of The Happy Valley Orphanage and other ministries in the state of Orissa, India. When I heard those words I began to pray and test the Spirit to see if that was indeed a calling for Christ Community Church World Missions. We were already involved in Jamaica, Haiti and Bolivia and were not sure if our organization could assume another country. We began to pray and wait upon the Lord. The answer soon came and it was in the affirmative! Yes! We were supposed to go to India and test the waters. This happened in February 2007.

The Lord was so gracious to me in forming a team of church leaders to travel to India for a time of crusades, revivals and conferences. This anointed team consisted of Pastors Chuck Evans, George Cooper and Mark Spaulding. This team came together with prayer, faith, unity and a love for India. We prayed that God would use us to teach and encourage the large number of pastors and church leaders who would be attending the conference where we would be speaking. We prayed, also, for the lost souls that would be attending the revivals and crusades. We left for India on March 15th.

This journey took more than 40 hours from the time we left Carmel, Indiana, and arrived in Happy Valley in Orissa. The journey was long and arduous, but we were driven by a similar call that the Wise Men received as they followed that "Star" that led them to Bethlehem. I am convinced that those Wise Men rode their camels from India and we were blessed to ride a jet from Indiana. We found Jesus in India and they found Him in Israel.

We were greeted in the Happy Valley Orphanage by more than 45 young male orphans. They sang for us and gave us warm hugs as we entered their compound. That was the beginning of our relationship with the beautiful children and adults in India. The next day was Sunday and I chose to remain behind at the orphanage rather than attending one of the mission churches. I wanted to connect with the boys in the orphanage who would be available during that day. It only took a smile and a beckon of my hands, plus several coloring books and crayons, to win their little hearts. I was blessed as they colored Bible pictures and would hurry to show me their art work. When that activity was ended I got lots of smiles, hugs and greetings in English that they had memorized. I had to remind myself that these young men were some of the poorest children in the world. They came from the lowest part of the caste system in India and that means that they have no privileges. Their families live in poverty and squalor. The lowest jobs in the nation are saved for them and the pay is pathetic. So many children are left orphans due to the lack of medical assistance and starvation. But, to watch them, listen to their excited voices and see their beautiful smiles one would never suspect that they were victims of poverty. These young men have been rescued by the Happy Valley Orphanage Mission. They now have hope. Their faces showed their joy and appreciation. They have been accustomed since birth to sleep on the floor, eat with their right hands, use the left one for toilet paper, wear whatever might be available and eat whatever might be available. In spite of all the suffering and dire poverty these children still carry an infectious smile.

Also, each of the young boys signed their names to the art work and wanted me to bring them back to America to show others these little gifts of their appreciation. During the art project we were joined by some of the ladies and men who work for the mission. One of the cooks was a Hindu and he and I bonded together that day. He couldn't wait to bring us cups of hot tea or coffee whenever he thought we might enjoy it. This was a great day in my life, but the next day, the pastors-leaders conference, was the highlight of the entire trip to India for me.

I was assigned to speak in the afternoon session of the pastors-leaders conference. I was not prepared for what happened. The conference was held under a canvas tabernacle stretched over a bamboo construction. The men were seated on the right side of the tabernacle and the women on the left. Most of the ladies and children sat on the ground. The ladies were dressed in the beautiful silk saris that gave them such a modest, biblical appearance. The music and singing began. In the typical India worship service it is expected that the service will last about three hours. We enjoyed this lively, rhythmic music. But, it appeared to me that there was a spirit of somber reserve. The Spirit seemed to be speaking to me to preach-teach on the topic of "Joy!" It was the best moment of the entire trip for me. We were all blessed by the response of these hundreds of precious, hungry-for-the-Spirit Indians. The invitation and challenge to "rejoice and be exceedingly glad" was greeted by spontaneous clapping, dancing and singing by the entire congregation. It was so contagious that the Americans were celebrating, also. One of the lady delegates to the conference, who was about 70 years old, left the audience and climbed up to the pulpit area and invited me to dance with her. What a joy! She danced me across the front of the pulpit while she celebrated the Joy of the Lord. Then, she moved to each of the American pastors and involved them in this colorful celebration. That day I knew that part of my heart would always be in India. From that day the miracles and joy increased.

We witnessed so many people responding to the invitations in the different services. Many came for special prayer for their own salvation while others were seeking healing of their bodies and for their families. Some days the conferences or crusades would last more than ten hours in the morning, afternoon and evening sessions! No one wanted to leave until the last amen had been spoken. In one crusade the people, more than 4,000, I think, had sat on the ground under a tabernacle of sticks, string and leaves for more than eight hours just waiting for the Americans to arrive from a distant destination. What patience and hunger for Christ.

Another highlight of joy was the moment when we were able to inspect the new property that has now been purchased in the name of Christ Community Church World Mission. These five acres will house the boarding school (free of course) for a lot of poor children and orphans. The vision includes not only dormitories for the children and the school facilities, but also a small medical center to attract the community to our school and church.

As we walked over the acreage that day and prayed for the new school and other facilities we could only rejoice that our Heavenly Father had called us more than 10,000 miles to this site to be a blessing to His children in India. The joy and the promises still continue to this day. We have been assured that the entire cost of these buildings have already been promised and provided! How can this be possible? It is very simple! His calling is His provision! He only asks us to hear and heed His voice and He will do the rest. Winona and I cannot wait to return to this beautiful land and those precious children where once more "we will dance for joy!"

Will you please pray for this area of India? In the past few weeks there have been terrible outbreaks of persecution against many of our churches and pastors. Around 100 churches have been burned, several pastors have been killed and many believers have had their homes destroyed. We have been able to open the orphanage in the State of Orissa in 2008. We believe that in spite of the heavy persecution that continues in this area of India that the gospel will continue to flow and many people will find Christ. Will you pray for all of the churches, orphanages, girls' homes and other ministries?

16

"Will You Take Our Baby Sister?"

There was a knock at our mission door one early morning in the tropical mountain country of Bolivia. When we answered the door that led to the street of that bustling village we saw a sight that deeply affected our lives.

Standing before us were two small Indian girls, both of them under 10 years old, and they were carrying a tiny baby in a basket. The baby had just been born and its little body had only been partially cleaned. The two little girls looked at me with sad countenances and said, "Señor, will you take our baby sister?" The young sisters continued with this heart-wrenching story.

"Last night our baby sister was born and our mama died! We have been trying to take care of our sister but we don't know how. We tried to give her some milk, but she doesn't want to take it." I looked at the bottle that was lying beside the tiny infant in the basket. It was a wine bottle and it was filled with cold milk. Winona and I felt a great wave of compassion for those three little homeless girls.

"We have some relatives out in the country where we can go and stay, but there is no one who will take our baby," the teary-eyed children continued. "Will you take our baby sister?" Winona and I looked at each other and made an instant decision. "Yes, we will take care of your baby sister!" The two little girls almost danced for joy as they handed their sister to us and said their farewells.

The first thing was to find a baby bottle and some warm milk for the precious little infant. Buena-Ventura, a teenager who lived with us, stepped forward and said, "I will take care of her." Soon the baby had been given a warm bath, a delicious bottle of milk and her own private baby bed. Most of all she had a new loving, caring teenage mother who would give her everything she needed.

The next thing that we did was to select a name for our new angel baby. After a short consideration we decided that we should name her Maria (Mary), after the mother of Jesus. We dedicated her to the Lord and prayed that she would grow up to be a true follower of Jesus. Maria was in for another great miracle.

A young American couple who worked with a mission made a few brief visits to our community to assist with a number of projects to help the poor Indians that lived in the mountains and valleys of that section of Bolivia. We soon became acquainted with this couple and discovered that they were unable to have children and had been praying for a baby. When they met Maria for the first time they fell in love with her. It was both a happy and sad day when these young American volunteers asked if they might adopt our baby Maria. We knew that this was the Lord's will and, soon, the papers were signed and we said our sad, but joyful, goodbyes.

We have not heard any news from Maria for over 50 years, but we believe that she is living somewhere in America. We have prayed for her many times. One day we believe that our beautiful little Maria will recognize us up in heaven and we will spend eternity celebrating the day when her two sisters asked that wonderful question: "Will you take our baby sister?"

17

Charlie Collins Had a Miracle at St. V's!

Today Charlie Collins serves as the Overseer for Christ Community Church World Mission in Haiti. He has also assisted with the mission work in Jamaica. For a number of years he was a vital leader of the Christ Community Church near Sheridan. Brother Charlie has not always been an active participant in the work of Christ. We can remember when he first moved to the Lamong community.

Charlie and Bunny Collins, and their family, first came to central Indiana in 1987. In the early years of his life he had lived in a rural section of Mississippi not too far from the famous river by that name. He first came to our church after being invited to a pork roast. Soon after, he and his family started to attend the services and during one pageant-sermon portraying Isaac being sacrificed on the altar by his father Abraham, Charlie Collins made the greatest decision on planet earth. Charlie came to the altar and began a new life that has affected so many people in Indiana, Jamaica and Haiti. But, we nearly lost this man of God in 1993. Only a miracle saved him from an untimely death.

Charlie had received some treatment in a rural hospital, where the physician had mistakenly mixed two medications, one of them morphine, that nearly destroyed his brain. Shortly after the treatment we noticed that his behavior had totally changed. On one occasion he just walked into the parsonage living room and lay down on the couch without saying a word. He crossed his arms over his chest and just stared at the ceiling. Earlier he made the sign-language gestures of "I love you!" We tried to talk and pray with our dear brother, but we soon realized that Charlie needed some high-tech analysis and he was taken to the St. Vincent's hospital in Carmel. During one process where the technicians needed him to get in bed he fought all of us and we were forced to wrestle him into security straps. Our hearts were aching for our brother as the specialist decided to move Charlie to the St. Vincent's Hospital on 86th Street. The examinations began. Soon the results of the tests came back to us with devastating news.

The two mixed prescriptions had affected Charlie's brain and it was beginning to shut down. Our hearts were broken as we heard the doctors in the ICU unit tell us that Bunny should begin making plans for his funeral in the very near future. I prayed fervently as I drove back to the Lamong church parsonage. I suddenly felt that we must take some action immediately if Charlie was to live through the night. I began to call the members and participants of the church, asking if all of us would be willing to pray an hour during the oncoming night and the next day. Soon we had volunteers who promised to come throughout the next 24 hours. They vowed to spend an hour praying for Charlie's life.

I will never forget going into the sanctuary at different hours of the night and seeing those precious prayer warriors as they were pleading for our dying friend. We heard no news from St. Vincent's during the night, but we received a phone call the next morning that turned our sorrow into joy. Here is what we were told later by Charlie Collins: "They had given me no hope! They all expected that I would die during the night, and even if I did survive my mind would never be normal. But, early the next morning I awoke in the ICU Ward and did not know where I was. I called for attendants and they were totally astonished. They began to call the medics, and they, too, were speechless."

Brother Charlie was not allowed to go home immediately following his miracle. He was kept for an additional two weeks for tests and observations and was released for two hours at a time. When Charlie returned to his work it was only for a couple of hours each day while he was on the road to complete recovery. Our church, Christ Community, celebrated that wonderful miracle that brought our dear brother from the edge of eternity to become a fine leader who would "touch many places in the world."

Since that day brother Charlie has served in many capacities as a missionary and church leader. He has made seven work mission trips to Jamaica and six journeys to Haiti as the "overseer" of our wonderful church and school near Port au Prince. We still laugh about the four different times we invited Charlie to go on a mission trip and each time he would respond, "I'm not interested in that kind of thing. I prefer to give money so that someone else can go!"

Today, there is a far different story. Charlie is a missionary with a great love for the poor lost children and adults of the Caribbean. He believes in miracles, also. The main reason is that Charlie Collins is a walking, talking miracle!

Section II

Some Miracle Voices
We Have Heard

Many people have questioned me about "hearing the voice" of the Lord. I am not sure if anyone can explain this wonderful miracle, but I am sure of one thing and that is, "He does speak to us!" In John 10:14, Jesus said, "I am the good shepherd, and know my sheep, and am known of mine…[v16] and other sheep I have, which are not of this fold: them also I must bring and they shall hear my voice…." I know Jesus as my Shepherd and I listen to His voice. To me it is miraculous, but also very simple. The most important thing for us to do is to simply walk close to His side and "listen to His still, small voice." This is one of the greatest truths that I have discovered. In the next few short stories I will share some of those special "voices" that we have heard. I am often asked if I hear His actual voice and I can only respond that it is not a loud audible voice. Most times it is a whisper in my mind or a strong feeling in my spirit. I try to be very careful to discern the difference between the voices of the "enemy," who comes to deceive, and the true voice of the Good Shepherd. I am totally convinced that we must seek the "gift of discernment" from the Holy Spirit to be able to discern the counterfeit from the authentic.

18

Tom Ditch Nearly Died!

Pastor Tom Ditch has been one of our favorite singers, pastors, writers and friends. At one time in our careers we planned to work together at a church where I was pastor, but it did not work out. Shortly after that Winona and I felt the call to move to Jamaica as missionaries.

Brother Tom has made mission trips to Jamaica and was deeply loved for his singing and kind, loving spirit. In fact, one of the Jamaican pastors named their new baby girl in honor of Tom. In the last few years things the Ditch family has experienced a great number of trials and tribulations. One of those nearly took the life of Pastor Ditch.

Tom had undergone a number of medical operations and treatments in recent years for his heart. As a matter of fact, his heart today is only operating at about five percent of its normal capacity. Outside of the surgeries, Pastor Ditch has suffered a serious motorcycle accident that crushed one of his legs. The pain following the surgeries became almost unbearable.

Also, the "enemy" has attacked Tom in a number of ways in recent years. One of those attacks came from church people that he loved and trusted. This left him deeply discouraged and bordering on depression. It seemed to Brother Tom that other friends had forsaken him, also. Then, to make things worse, he had to face enormous financial indebtedness following the high number of surgeries and medical treatments. Then, the motorcycle accident happened and that left him broken physically, financially, emotionally and spiritually. It seemed that he had been abandoned by everyone.

Brother Tom faced some of the hardest battles that he had ever known. The pain intensified and even the morphine pills were not effective. His mind was constantly attacked by thoughts such as, "God doesn't love me any more!" "My family doesn't need me anymore!" "My friends have all forsaken me!" "I just want to die!" Tom had to deal with those horrible mental, physical and spiritual attacks every day and night. It seemed that there was no hope. Finally, Tom decided that he could not endure it any longer. The torture from the pain of his crushed leg was intolerable. Not even one morphine tablet an hour was able to control Pastor Tom's agony. Tom decided to end it all that very night.

He was unable to cope with all the torment that was wracking his body and mind. He felt that the only solution was to take an overdose of those powerful morphine capsules. In the midst of that black night of horror our precious pastor took one hundred morphine tablets. No one could possibly survive that amount of pain killers. Soon, Tom felt himself drifting into another dimension. He was now free from the physical world that he had always known, but he still carried a heavy burden of pain. Our precious brother moved through an ethereal cloud and soon arrived at his destination. He recognized that this was a part of God's Kingdom, but he had no idea how to enter in. He saw guards on the great walls of this city and he asked them if he might enter in.

The armed guards on the high walls looked at Tom and gave him a disappointing answer. "You cannot enter this kingdom. It is not your time. You still have something else to accomplish!" Brother Tom Ditch tried to get an explanation as to why he could not enter. The answers were always the same. Finally some relief came.

A door opened from the walls of the city and a young lady with dark brown hair came out and walked towards Tom. She knew him and called him by name. He was not sure whether she was a family member that had died several years before or if she was an angel. She said words that brought great joy to our brother who still carried a heavy load of pain and suffering. "Tom, go take off your shoes and put your feet in the river!" This turned out to be a glorious experience.

As he put his broken, bruised and pain-riddled feet in that river all of his agony lifted. He was free! He was full of joy as that celestial river took away the pain in his feet and legs that had suffered so long. Then, the beautiful lady spoke to him again: "Tom, take a drink of the water from the river!" When he drank the water from that River of Life he felt all of his pain, anxiety, depression and sadness leave his body. Now, he was totally free! He never wanted to leave this place. He felt like a brand new man. Then, the angelic lady gave him some words of disappointment. She said, "Tom, you have to go back home! There is still one more thing that you must do before you come back here."

Brother Tom tried to persuade the "angel" to let him stay, since he did not believe that he could tolerate the life he had known before. Finally, Pastor Tom agreed to those terms and he felt his spirit re-entering his body. He awakened to discover that he was now back in his home and that much of his pain was gone. In fact, Tom experienced the same dream four nights in a row. His biggest dilemma was, "What is it that I am supposed to do before I can return to my heavenly home?" This was a puzzling question. Then, the answer came.

The Lord revealed to Tom that he was to do one more musical CD and that he was to donate it to Christ Community Church World Missions! He definitely felt that this would be a great blessing to him and that it would assist with the missions of Jamaica, Haiti, Bolivia and India. But, how would he find the money to do a CD? He was already carrying a very heavy financial burden. The answer came through a phone call. I felt that I was supposed to call my friend, Pastor Tom, and ask him how we might be able to help him. His answer was, "pray for me that I will be able to do one more CD before I die. I want to donate it to the Mission." I told him that I would pray about it and share the dream with others. I had no idea what I would hear when I told our Board of Directors a few days after that phone conversation.

The Board of Directors met a few days after I had talked with Tom and I shared the "out of body experience" and the desire for "one more CD!" I was overwhelmed with the rush of enthusiasm from our directors. "How much will he need for the CD?" I had checked with Pastor Tom and he told me that it would cost $5,000. He had no idea where that money might come from. The Christ Community Church Board of Directors responded immediately. Within a matter of minutes the entire amount had been pledged. I couldn't wait to tell my dear brother.

Within a few days the CD project began. Another miracle happened as the rush of faith and enthusiasm flooded Brother Tom's mind and body. "God still loves me and wants to use me!" Those were some of the thoughts that rekindled and renewed Tom. He was a new man. He had a divine purpose. The dream had come true.

On June 9th, Pastor Tom not only presented his new album at our Christ Community Church World Mission Spring Festival, but, also he sang before an enthralled audience. What a joy! His mission was completed! He was now free to go or stay! Will each of you say a prayer for Brother Tom as he bears his cross of pain and suffering?

I believe, that one day, when we all get to heaven, we will see brother Tom rejoicing in his new body, free from all the trials and tribulations, and we will hear him sing one of my favorites, "The Old Rugged Cross Made the Difference" or "Peace in the Midst of the Storm."

19

Winona Entered into the Holy of Holies!

Winona tells this story:

I was worshipping at one of the church services in Golden Grove, Jamaica. The music and singing were loud that day. When it came time for prayer it seemed that the entire congregation prayed together. That is a beautiful custom among many of our churches, but on that occasion I needed to hear the "still small voice" of my Shepherd. I tried to concentrate my prayer, but the praise and worship was too loud on that occasion. I asked my Heavenly Father this special request: "Father, may I come into the Holy of Holies, today?"

A wonderful thing happened at that moment. I had never seen anything like that before. I was instantly ushered into the Holy Presence of the Father and His Son, Jesus. I was in the Holy of Holies! My soul was filled with rapturous joy. I saw Jesus sitting on His throne. I did not see the face of the Father, but I did see His hand as He placed it on the shoulder of Jesus, and I heard the Father say: "It's almost time, my Son!"

I realized that the Holy Father was referring to the Return of Christ to the earth to rapture His church. Then, Jesus looked at the Father and said, "But, there are so many who are not ready, My Father." I waited in complete awe and anticipation for the Father's answer. There were no other words spoken. I was instantly transferred back into the Christ Community Church worship service in Golden Grove, Jamaica. My heart was pounding with the joy and excitement of having had such a rapturous moment in the presence of the Trinity. I knew that I would never be the same. But, what did those words spoken by the Father signify? I asked my husband after the worship services had ended.

My husband and I could not discern or interpret the meaning of that glorious announcement. We did, however, come to this conclusion: Jesus is coming soon! Many will not be ready! We must teach and warn everyone that He is coming soon! The Father has set the date! I hope and pray that each of us will be ready!

20

"Go Tell That Sailor!"

I was the evangelist in a crusade in Terre Haute, Indiana, back in the 1960s. My father-in-law, Pastor Tom Moody, Winona's dad, was a member to the Terre Haute Southside Church of the Nazarene, where the revival was underway. It was on Sunday night, I believe, and we had a nice attendance. I remember that Dr. Leo Davis, superintendent of the Southwest Indiana District of the Church of the Nazarene, was in attendance.

The audience had been very attentive and the Spirit had led me to speak on the theme of repentance and salvation. As I completed the message, the music began and a song of invitation was given. A few people came forward and knelt at the altar. I noticed a young sailor standing with a group of young people in the back of the audience. Suddenly I felt a strong compulsion to go back to the young sailor and invite him personally to come forward for prayer. I could not remember ever having done it that way before. I knew I must go! It was like a voice in my spirit that prompted me to walk slowly in the direction of that handsome young military man. I reached out to touch his shoulder. He quickly walked away from me toward the side aisle and moved very swiftly toward the altar. He knelt down and began to confess his sins and invite Jesus into his heart. After the prayer session was over each person stood to give a testimony of his or her commitment to Christ. The young sailor gave this exciting testimony. "I did not believe in a real God," he spoke in an emotional tone.

"As the message was given and the invitation started I said, 'God if you are real send that preacher to me and let him ask me to go to that altar!' I now know that He is real and I am going to serve Him." We all celebrated that night at the Southside Church of the Nazarene.

We were so thankful for everyone who came forward that night to receive Christ into their hearts. I was especially thrilled that I had listened to "The Shepherd's Voice." Remember, He still speaks to each of us, His sheep, "in that still small voice."

21

"Change Your Sermon!"

I had been asked to preach at a revival near Boise, Idaho. The crusade had gone well and we were preparing for the final service on a Sunday night. I had prepared an inspirational, encouraging message for those who had made decisions during the meetings that week. Also, I felt the need to give some words to bless the local church members and leaders. The time for the evening service was drawing near. The following day I would be flying back to Indiana. Then, I heard "that voice"! I knew that it was my Shepherd and that I must obey in order to have His blessings. In my spirit I felt that I must preach a sermon on Hell. I felt a spirit of dread since I had not spoken on that subject for a long time. It didn't seem to make sense to me. But, I knew that I had heard the voice and I must obey.

As I spoke that evening there was a strong spirit of conviction in the audience. Other voices seem to taunt me, saying, "This message will turn the people off. It will be offensive to them! What will the church leaders think?" I had to deal with an admixture of voices that special evening in Idaho.

As I gave the invitation that evening a number of people came to the altars to repent of sins; to make new commitments to Christ; or to seek directions in their lives. One young lady made a special decision about her eternal destiny that evening. Following the service I was introduced to her as "the daughter of the lieutenant governor of the State of Idaho!" It was, perhaps the only message that could have reached her heart. We celebrated all of those who came to Christ that evening, but I rejoiced in that I had heard His voice and obeyed. Heaven celebrated that night, also.

22

Little Stephen Helped
Save an Airplane

I believe that little children many times hear the voice of the Lord better than most adults do. I know of so many instances when children's prayers saved our lives or delivered us from some crisis. Little Jacob Bush and his young preschool "buddies" felt the need to pray that God would stop the hurricane in Jamaica and it happened! I can remember so many instances when children prayed and miracles happened. This is such a story.

We were returning to Indiana following a four-year mission to Chile and Bolivia, South America. We had seen so many marvelous miracles during that era. Now, we were returning to Indiana, where I would be going back to the universities for some needed degrees that would enable us to do ministries in the Westfield schools and the churches in Hamilton County. Also, these diplomas would open so many doors for us to minister in places such as China, Russia and other places where missionaries were forbidden. But, now we were seated in an airplane as it taxied slowly to the runway that would fly us from Lima, Peru, to another airport in Nicaragua and then on to Miami, Florida, where family would be waiting for us. Then... something went wrong! "Papa! Papa! Algo esta mal con este avion!" It was the voice of our 2-year-old son, Stephen, as he cried out above the sound of the racing engines that were now almost ready to race down the airstrip and would climb upwards above the Pacific Ocean, and fly us northwards over Central America, Cuba and into Miami. "Daddy, Daddy! Something is wrong with this airplane!" shouted our little 2-year-old son in Spanish. He was now crying in distress. What could it mean? The pilots were not aware of anything as they reminded us to buckle our seatbelts in preparation for take-off.

I knew that something was wrong. I felt the same "panic" for prayer that Stephen felt, so we began to pray. The DC-4 shivered as the propellers accelerated in readiness for the dash down the runway. The plane continued to wait. We kept right on praying. Then, the Panagra airliner began to move! It began to gather speed! Then, we felt the brakes being applied and it came to a complete halt. What was wrong? The pilot soon gave us this notice. One of the engines had failed at that moment. We would have to return to the airport and wait for about 4–5 hours for a new engine. Had this failure happened 10 seconds later the plane, we were told, could not have completed the take-off and we would have, most likely, fallen into the surging tides of the Pacific Ocean.

Within a few minutes we were given permission to disembark from the crippled airplane and to spend some time visiting in the city of Lima. We were all so blessed and joyful as we drove around that ancient city of the Incas. We knew that the Lord had spared us that day and we believed that another miracle had happened when Stephen heard the voice of his Shepherd. I am reminded of this miracle almost every time we are preparing for a "take-off" to some country in the world.

23

"Wait at the Flooded Airport!"

His name was Max Greene. He was a special friend who worked with us in Bolivia back in the 1950s. Max was assigned to the Riberalta, Bolivia, jungle areas. I was so blessed to have the opportunity to introduce him to a number of the jungle communities along the Beni and Madre De Dios rivers that flowed into the mighty Amazon. Max and Leslie, his wife, came to Bolivia from Boston and were not accustomed to the rugged conditions of that part of South America. I thought it was rather humorous to see Max meticulously place tiny band-aids over dozens of mosquito bites over his body.

When it came time to sleep that first night in a jungle "hotel" room, Max was very careful to make sure that his mosquito netting was tucked in at every corner. He did not want to sleep with those pesky critters. The next morning I looked over at Max sleeping on that hard mattress in a room that was more than 85 degrees and I saw something that caught my eye. There were no mosquitoes in bed with Max, but clinging to the inside of his netting was a very large, poisonous spider that measured more than six inches long. You can only imagine the excitement when I woke him up to show him his bed-mate.

Another time we had a big laugh after I had talked to a couple of the natives in their language and Max was so eager to find out what they were saying and why they kept looking at him. I was only teasing when I told him that they were cannibals and they were trying to decide which of us they would like to eat. Max didn't always enjoy my sense of humor. But, Max soon became a seasoned missionary and prayer warrior. It was amazing to see his faith. He had been brought up in the Quaker faith, but he had never been exposed to such great challenges and prayer needs as he encountered in the

77

tropics of Bolivia. On one occasion he was visiting with us when we lived in Eagletown and ministering at the Eagle Creek Evangelical Friends Church, and Winona mentioned that her washing machine was broken.

Max asked Winona if he could go down in the basement of the parsonage and look at it. She readily consented, since we did not have money to repair the old one or buy a new one. Winona had tried to start the old washer several times, but had given up on it. Max walked over to the washing machine and laid his hands on it and began to pray. She had never seen anyone pray for a washer before. When Max finished his prayer he asked her to "try it again!" Winona turned the button and the machine started instantly. She was elated. The machine lasted for a long time after that. Max was a man of prayer.

One day, while serving in the jungle country of Bolivia, Max was praying to the Lord about needed funds for the mission and about returning to Indiana. He had been down in Bolivia for a number of years and it was time to go back to America to see about raising funds and promoting the mission. The main problem on this particular day was that a major flood had covered the entire region. There were no airplanes landing on that little grassy airport. There were no roads or trails open. The rivers had overflowed due to the torrential rains and the village of Riberalta, where Max lived, was under several inches of water. Max heard the voice of the Lord saying to him, "Go to the airport and wait for your plane to America!" That was humanly impossible! Max packed his two suitcases and waded out to the airport. It was closed!

Max was met by an official at the inundated airport and was told, "The airport is closed! There have been no planes since the flood and there are none scheduled! You will have to go back home!" Max answered the official with these words, "I will wait!" The custodian repeated the same words and looked in astonishment as Max waded out toward the flooded runway carrying two suitcases. Max stood there that day praying and trusting the Great Shepherd who had whispered to His obedient sheep a message that was hard to believe. Max waited and prayed. Then, he heard the sound of an airplane! The airport official shouted, "A plane is coming!" How would it land on that inundated airport? Then, they realized that a miracle was happening. It was an amphibious plane and it was from the US Air Force!

When the plane landed one of the Air Force officers waded across the landing strip and spoke with Max. This was not a scheduled landing place, but the U.S. Air Force had been deployed to assist with any emergency needs in that disaster area of South America. Within a few minutes Max had been welcomed aboard the military plane and was on his way to America. What a joy he must have felt that day that he prayed and listened to that wonderful voice of the Master of wind, waves, storms and floods of life. I hope and pray that you and I will become great prayer warriors and, also great "listeners" to our Heavenly "Abba!" (Papa).

24

The Wrong Hospital Room and the Wrong Name

Many times during our 50-plus years of ministry we have been asked to go visit someone's family member in the hospital, nursing home or at their home. On this particular occasion we were given the name of "Mary Jones" (not her actual name, of course). I was told that she was in the Riverview Hospital and that she quite ill and was not a Christian. I'm sure that I was told the correct room number, also, but sometimes a memory loss can prove to be a blessing. In this case it was.

I went to the room that I thought was the right one. I spoke to the lady in the bed and told her who I was. I called her by the name, "Mary," and she responded properly to that name. After a few moments of introductory comments I asked if I could pray for her. She readily agreed to my request. I asked her, also, if she would like to receive Christ as her Savior and she responded in the affirmative. We went through the steps of salvation and prayed the Sinner's Prayer together. She seemed so happy that she had entered into a new relationship. Then, I congratulated Mary and prepared to leave. I said to her, "Mary, it is so nice to have met you and I pray that you will continue in your faith!" and similar phrases. Mary looked at me and said, "My name is not Mary! Mary is in the next room!" I was shocked and overjoyed when I went into the "real Mary's" room, where we had another miracle prayer time.

25

The Voice at Cool Lake Golf Course

I had been the high school golf coach at Westfield for a number of years. The last year that I served in that capacity our team won the Range Line Conference Championship. At that time I felt that golf had a therapeutic value, in that it offered exercise and relaxation. At that stage of my life I enjoyed the competition as well. One of my favorite hobbies during those years was to search for lost golf balls. It turned out to be productive as I gathered hundreds of balls that had strayed into the woods, roughs and even shallow water hazards. All of these events happened during our ministry at Eagle Creek plus teaching science at the Westfield Middle School.

When I retired from teaching and coaching at Westfield, we were able to open a new church in Lamong, near Sheridan, and Winona named it Christ Community Church. I fully intended to continue my hobby of playing golf and searching for golf balls. To me it was a challenge, in that I had trained my "reticular activator" (a section of the brain) to assist me in seeing golf balls that, perhaps, other people could not see. One day I was playing golf and searching for golf balls when I heard that Precious Still Voice of my Shepherd. I can never explain this to others, but I know that "whisper impression" in my spirit that is unmistakable!

I was playing the 10th hole, I think, at a golf course called Cool Lake. I had hit my drive down the fairway and was waiting for the golfers ahead of me to finish their putts. During those few moments I strolled over into the rough, under some shade trees, to look for lost balls. It was there that I heard the voice that changed my life. The voice said to my heart-spirit, "Jack, I will teach you how to win souls the way you find lost golf balls!" Wow! I nearly weep every time I recall that moment! Find souls? Our churches had always been growing churches. We had seen lots of new people come to Christ over the years in Chile, Bolivia and America as missionaries and pastors. Now, we were being promised a more fruitful ministry. That day at Cool Lake golf course my life was changed. I became a seeker of "sheep" and I had to put my golf clubs and golf balls into storage or give them away. But, how would it work? What was I to do differently? The answer soon came.

The Lord revealed to me that I must find a lot of helpers for this new and challenging ministry. I began to teach and preach that the main purpose of our church would be what Jesus taught Peter in John 21:15–17. After Christ's resurrection, He found Peter in Galilee, where he had gone back to his old trade as a fisherman. Jesus prepared breakfast for the disciples that day and asked Peter one of the greatest questions in history: "Do you truly love me?" When Peter answered in the affirmative three times, Jesus said to him these life-changing challenges: "Feed my lambs," "Take care of my sheep" and "Feed my sheep." Wow! I was hearing something similar.

One of our first techniques at Christ Community Church following that encounter on the golf course was to recruit a lot of prayer partners. Then, I announced to the church that we would all pray during the week that we would be able to find lost sheep. This could take the form of personal evangelism in jails, hospitals, nursing homes, door to door and, of course through the invitations we would extend to the lost or straying sheep that came to our services. We decided that we would have a celebration each Sunday morning and light a candle for each new "sheep" that was found that week. We would then have the entire congregation stand and rejoice and celebrate each name that was introduced.

At first the numbers were pretty scarce, but we continued to pray. We opened a special prayer meeting each week for people to come and intercede for lost friends and family. We had people coming to the church altars during the day to pray an hour. Soon we began to see the harvest. Every Sunday, I believe, new converts were listed and celebrated. Mission teams began to spread out to Jamaica, Mexico,

Kentucky, Indianapolis and other areas and they would bring back glowing reports of people being saved and baptized. Then, Winona and I heard the voice telling us that we must leave America and go to the "white harvest fields" of Russia, China, Jamaica and other parts of the world.

I'm so glad that I heard "the voice" that day on the golf course at Cool Lake. We are both so excited and thrilled to have helped the Great Shepherd find some of His lost sheep in four colors in many nations. We give Him all the glory! I believe the key is to pray, listen to "the voice of The Great Shepherd," and go where He leads His sheep-shepherds like us. Remember! The angels rejoice when one soul comes to Christ!

26

"Put It All in the Plate Tonight!"

Winona and I were students in the Union Bible School in Westfield, Indiana, at the time. Our schedules were very busy with school, plus I was employed at RCA Victor on the 3:00–11:30 p.m. shift. On Sunday mornings and evenings we assisted with a small evangelical mission located in one of the storefront buildings in Fishers, Indiana. It was exciting because I had the opportunity to share the Word from time to time. We were not certain, at that time, as to what the future might hold for us, although we hoped that, someday, we might be able to do missionary work.

The finances during those days were very scarce. Sometimes we did not have enough to buy food after paying our tuition, rent and other expenses. On one occasion we ate almost nothing but tomato soup for over one month. Someone had given us a couple of cases of that delicious sauce. I even took it in my lunch bucket to work. We refused to go into debt, as we felt that it was not a scriptural thing to do at that time. One of the main things that we always had to watch in our budget was gas expenses for our car, since I had to drive to Indianapolis every night to work. Then, one night we were given a major test of our faith. I heard the "inner voice" say to me, as the offering plate was being passed in the Sunday evening service, "Put it all in the offering!"

That was a shocking moment, since most of that money was reserved for gas and other car expenses for the next week. What could we do? I emptied my billfold into the offering plate and my mind was filled with a series of questions. Did I hear the voice? How will I get to work next week? Will I lose my job? We drove back to Westfield with many questions, but also praying that He would see us through our dilemma. It was now late in the evening. In a few minutes we would go to bed. Would I be able to sleep? The next morning we would have classes all morning and then I would prepare for my job, located on east Michigan Street in Indianapolis. Then, we heard a knock on the door of our tiny apartment. Who could be knocking at that time of the evening?

When I opened the door I instantly recognized another student of the Union Bible College. He was holding something in his hand and stretching it in my direction. "The Lord told me to bring this to you tonight!" he said.

We could not believe our eyes as we accepted that precious gift from the Lord. It was more than enough money to get us through the next week until payday.

I sincerely believe that this "miracle" was the beginning of a lifetime of hearing and obeying His voice. We rejoiced that night that we had obeyed the voice of the Savior and had witnessed that miracle of provision. We have heard that "still small voice" throughout our 56 years of marriage and we can testify that He never fails! We hope that you, too, will listen and obey our wonderful Shepherd.

27

Coach Jim Beery Saw a Miracle at the Olympics

Coach Jim Beery has always been a model Christian football coach in my eyes. For a number of years this dedicated teacher, parent and coach has helped mold countless lives through his involvement with young athletes at North Knox High School in southern Indiana.

Jim has also been involved in Sunday school and church in his community. Jim and his wonderful wife, Merry, are the parents of two children. One of them, Daniel, was a member of the USA Rowing Team in the 2004 Olympics, which were held in Athens, Greece. I will never forget receiving an e-mail from Jim after that event telling me that Daniel's team had won and that he believed that he had witnessed a miracle. He reminded me, also, that he had read our first book, *Miracles We Have Seen,* and that it inspired him to pray for a miracle in Athens. Here is the account of that miraculous day when God stopped the wind and gave a "level playing field" for both the USA and Canada. Here is Coach Jim Beery's account of that unforgettable day.

> I have always held fast to the scripture that promises Jesus is the same yesterday, today, and tomorrow, and always. In August of 2004 we found lodging in the little town of Marathonis, about twenty-six miles from Athens, close to the Aegean Sea. We lived for ten days in an apartment above a Greek restaurant, located about two miles from the rowing venue.
>
> On the morning of the initial racing competition, I arose early and went out on the veranda for my quiet time devotions. Only the sound of roosters crowing off in the distance could be heard. (Greek roosters, by the way, crow in the same language as American roosters). I soon learned that the Greeks party late

86

and sleep late, so there was an amazing quietness surrounding me that morning. Yet, I felt uneasiness, because the racing course was notorious for the rough waters when the relentless winds came in from the sea. In fact, the previous summer, during the Junior Olympics competition, the waves actually swamped some of the boats, endangering the crews.

I had no particular scriptures in mind that morning, so I just opened my little *Good News for Modern Man* Bible at random. On the page in front of me was the figure of a boat in a storm. The Scriptures were Mark 4:35–42. The disciples were terrified by the storm, and awoke Jesus, saying, "...don't you care that we are about to drown?" Jesus quieted the winds and told the sea to be still. As I read those words I asked myself, "If Jesus could quiet the winds and the rough waters back then, why could He not do it this very day?" So, that was my prayer that morning. I knew Dan's "eight" was a fast boat, and they had a good chance to upset the highly favored Canada team if the conditions were right.

When we met at the bus stop for our ride to the racing course, one of the rower's mothers asked me, "Aren't you terribly nervous this morning?" I smiled at her and replied, "Everything is going to be all right. I have been praying this morning."

Early in the racing schedule, it was apparent that the winds were increasingly strong and the water was becoming rougher. Little whitecaps began to form on the surface. During preparations for the Olympics, giant JumboTron displays were installed on both sides of the course, so fans could look across to the other side to watch the race on the giant screens from the beginning to the finish line. However, on the opposite side of the course from us, the JumboTron interfered with the timing devices at the finish line, so it was dismantled, and we could not view the start and early stages of the races. Some of our fans actually walked around to the opposite side of the venue to watch the race on the JumboTron placed on our side of the course.

Dan's heat race that morning was the final race of the day. Kate, one of the rower's girlfriends, had gone across to the other side of the venue to watch the entire race on the one JumboTron. She was unaware of my prayers, but after the race she commented to us, "It was just amazing. All morning the officials had trouble getting the boats lined up quietly for the start, because the water was so rough. But, when the 'eights' lined up, the water seemed to quiet down!"

Although we could not see the early action, we listened to the race commentary on the loudspeakers. First the race was announced in Greek, and then in English. The powerful Canadian boat took an early lead, as expected. However, the USA boat remained well within contention. For over two years the Canadians had been unchallenged and no opposing boat had "rowed through" them.

With less than 500 meters to go, the boats passed our viewing area. I could feel my skin tingle, and Merry began to tug at my arm. "Jim, I think we are gaining on the Canadians!"

As both boats neared the finish line, the bright blue boat with the red, white and blue oars surged ahead. Amazing! The announcer called out the winning boat, "…the United States of America has upset the highly favored Canadians, AND they have broken the world record!"

That morning Dan's boat rowed the 2,000-meter race faster than any boat in the history of the Olympics. This victory enabled the crew to rest and train at leisure, while the Canadians and other boats had to come back in the middle of the week for more qualifying racing. Oh, one problem! At the end of the eight's race, the winds became so strong and the waves so fierce, the course was closed down for about the next thirty-six hours!

The following Sunday was an incredibly beautiful day. Once again the eights were the final race of the day. Up to that point the USA men had not won a gold medal. I listened closely as the announcer excitedly called out the race. Particularly, I was interested in how the boats were doing at the 500-meter mark, because Dan had confided in me the previous day, "Dad, the coach has changed his strategy for tomorrow's race. He wants us to attempt a 'breakaway' move at the 500 meters mark and try to distance ourselves from the field—to make the others chase us all the way."

And, it was at about that point that the incredulous announcer exclaimed, "…the USA boat has put on an amazing burst of speed, what power, and has achieved 'open water' between themselves and the rest of the crews."

It has been termed the most dominant race by an eight in the history of Olympic rowing. Although the Dutch boat made a valiant effort in the last 100 meters, they could not close on the bright-blue USA boat. For the first time in nearly forty years, gold medals were placed around the necks of eight American rowers and their coxswain, the National Anthem was played, and the stars and stripes were unfurled above all others."

Tears clouded my eyes, and I shook my head in amazement, saying to myself, "Thank you, dear God." The same God, yesterday, today, tomorrow and forever!

This is an amazing story of faith and prayer. Our God is able to stop the winds and waves for all of us as we run our races and fight our fights. I hope that we will all learn this precious lesson from Coach Jim Beery, who called on his Heavenly Father that day in Athens, Greece, and asked for a special favor. I can't wait to see the gold medal that Dan Beery won that day. I hope, also, that each of you will stand in the winner's circle one day and hear Him say, "Well done!"

28

Evangelist James Tharp Had a Miracle in Santa Cruz

Rev. James Tharp is, in my opinion, one of the top evangelists in the world. We are honored to have known Pastor J.W. for more than 50 years. Our dear brother has served a number of powerful churches across America during that time. He is the author of a number of books and teaching materials. He is the founder of an International Prayer Ministry Teaching Seminar that has impacted a number of nations. He also has been closely affiliated with Rev. Billy Graham and other prominent ministers and evangelists. During the past seven years, J.W. has been a great blessing to us in Jamaica, Haiti and Bolivia as our Evangelist and School of Prayer Instructor.

A little more than a year ago, Rev. Tharp went through a powerful crisis in his life, due to the death of his precious wife of more than fifty years, Maxine. She was such a strength and blessing to J.W., and her loss left him saddened and in some depression. It was during those moments of heartbreak and mental pain that Pastor Tharp came to assist us in Santa Cruz, Bolivia, with a Crusade and a School of Prayer. I will never forget his arrival to our school campus located on the edge of our tropical city.

Brother Tharp was very tired following his lengthy journey to South America. We could see in his face the effects of the recent great loss in his life. Also, he revealed to us later that he was suffering from severe symptoms of diabetes. But, God had a prescription waiting for this great warrior of the cross. He was about to feel the effects of God's *agape* love being shared by the children and leaders of Christ Community Church in Bolivia.

They were waiting outside the school building. There were more than 140 children and teachers lined up in the road to sing songs of welcome to Pastor J.W. Tharp and each one would give him a hug and a kiss on the cheek. This type of therapy continued throughout the nearly two weeks that J.W. was with us. We could see the joy being restored to our wonderful leader and we rejoiced with him. And, there was more to come.

Each night Rev. Tharp preached in different churches across our city. His messages were powerful and many came forward to receive salvation, The Holy Spirit, healing and other blessings. The people of Santa Cruz loved brother J.W.

Each day, for more than two hours, Brother Tharp taught many of our teachers, pastors and leaders the principles of prayer in his world renowned School of Prayer Seminar. This was a great time of training for our leaders. It was also a time of Miracle for Rev. J.W.

On the last day of our seminar a number of people had come forward for the "laying on of hands" as they brought their prayer requests to the altar. I felt a very strong compulsion to ask our pastors and leaders to lay hands on Brother Tharp for his healing and blessings. This resulted in a wonderful miracle for J.W. He wrote to us later, "I went to my physician for a scheduled examination and to begin my diabetes treatment with the high dosage insulin injections. After my doctor examined me he stated that I my blood count was low and I would not need the insulin." We all rejoiced when we heard about that miracle. Also, Pastor Tharp wrote to us following his Crusade and Prayer Seminar in Bolivia that he was no longer depressed. The hugs, kisses, love and prayers of the children had healed him!

But, there was one more miracle that happened while our dear evangelist was with us in Santa Cruz. It happened a day or so following those ministries. It was early in the morning and I was praying in the large patio adjacent to our mission house and school. Our worship services for the past year had been conducted outside under a large shade tree, or in the event of rain we brought the folding chairs under the long porches of the rented mission building.

As I walked and prayed that morning, I felt the Spirit leading me to pray for the property where I was walking. This was a large, beautiful courtyard filled with palm trees, flowers and playgrounds for the children. It had been loaned to us by a wealthy neighbor. We had requested, more than once, if we might be allowed to build a tabernacle on the property. Each time we were told that it would be impossible.

Nevertheless, as I walked that morning and prayed I felt that God was going to give us a miracle. I called Pastor J.W. Tharp and we both agreed to walk, pray and claim the property. When we finished our time of prayer we both felt that a "miracle" had happened. I went to the school office to call our school director, Karina Luna, to tell her of our impressions. As I explained to her in Spanish what we had just done she responded with a shout of joy. She replied, "I felt that I should go and talk to the owner of the property, also! The owner has given us permission to build a structure for church and school," she exulted.

In a few minutes our director arrived on campus and we all celebrated this wonderful news. Within a few days we had begun the "tabernacle" on that sacred property. Winona and I left for Indiana shortly after the project began. We received the wonderful news a couple of weeks later that the tabernacle had been completed and the school had held its first "preschool graduation" a few days later. At this moment it is being used on a daily basis for school and church activities. Thank you, Jesus! Also, special thanks to Pastor James Tharp for his faithfulness in coming to Santa Cruz to help us claim those miracles!

29

A Miracle in Cuba

Prayer was our main ministry while living in Jamaica during the 90s and the early part of the 21st century. We were involved in directing churches, schools, and one small orphanage, plus teaching in the Cornerstone Christian Academy, yet we recognized very early that there were mighty battles to fight. We had experienced so many attacks from the enemy all across the island where we have churches and schools. We knew that we were wrestling "not against flesh and blood, but against the rulers, against the authorities, against the powers of this dark world" (Ephesians 6:12).

Each morning I would rise early to pray. There were prayer walks across the mountains with our dogs. There were other precious hours of prayer in the plastic chairs stationed over the mountainside plus the treehouse at the top. Some of the time we would just walk, praise and listen to the "still small voice" of the Good Shepherd. This is one of the greatest things I have learned in our ministries around the world. On one of those days I heard in my spirit a very different kind of message. I could hardly believe what I was feeling. I had a powerful impression in my mind that Winona and I must go to Cuba.

This message kept tugging at my mind and I knew that we must hear and heed the voice of the Shepherd. We knew of the problems we might face on that communist island. Furthermore, we did not have any contacts anywhere in Cuba. The "enemy" whispered many doubts into my mind in the next weeks as I tried to focus on that vision and calling of the Holy Spirit.

I discovered first of all that is not permitted for Americans to travel from the USA to Cuba. However, Cuba will allow U.S. citizens to enter from other ports of call without stamping their passports. This caused some consternation in our minds, in that we did not wish to disobey USA policies, yet we knew that God's voice has precedence over all of man's laws. We began to make plans to travel to that communist island ruled by Fidel Castro. What would we do there? Where would we stay? The enemy mocked us and whispered many doubts into our hearts. We contacted a travel agency in Jamaica and Cuba to begin our plans. We were aware that we might have to deal with American officials if our credentials were stamped in Cuba.

Winona and I flew to Havana, Cuba, and traveled by taxi more than fifty miles along the northern coast to a small city where we had made prior reservations. We found the people in the large hotel to be very hospitable and they greeted us with open arms. But, why were we there? What was the real purpose of this journey of blind faith? We had no idea other than that we had "heard the voice."

Oftentimes during the next three days I felt the call in my spirit to walk along the oceanfront and just pray for Cuba. I prayed for Fidel Castro and his cruel communist government. I prayed for the house churches that had sprung up all over Cuba since atheism had torn down the infrastructure of the traditional churches. Some house churches had disobeyed the strict regulations of the Cuban government and were bringing hundreds of people into their fellowship instead of the small number that had been mandated. One house church had more than 3,000 people meeting and worshipping on their grounds. The Cuban police had the pastor incarcerated. The entire community rose up in protest and marched against the local police station. He was released. But, persecution persisted all across Cuba.

After a few days of praying along beaches, roads and even in Havana, Winona and I returned to Jamaica. The one question that kept pounding in our minds was, "Why did you go to Cuba?" We could only focus on the voice that we had heard. We did not know why, but we did know that we had followed the Good Shepherd. We had obeyed our God. We knew that one day we would get the answer. Then…the answer came! We were blessed beyond words. Here is part of that miracle story.

I had worked previously in two former communist nations, the former Soviet Union and Belarus. We had received invitations to teach Russian teachers from the Bible in large convocations in many parts of Russia. We had been allowed to give large quantities of Bibles to teachers plus *Jesus* films and other materials for students. We had seen Russian teachers come to Christ in the very schools where atheistic communism had been taught previously. We had also worked in Red China with ELIC (English Language in China) and had seen many young people turn to Christ. Now...it was about to happen in Cuba!

The very days that Winona and I were in Cuba, some of the top leaders of ministries such as Campus Crusade, the Jesus Film Project and Walk through the Bible had been invited to meet with Fidel Castro. Following that session Fidel made a promise to those Christian ministry leaders that "I will not persecute the Christians in Cuba anymore!" This was one of the most shocking and blessed statements that had ever come from the dictator's lips. We rejoiced and celebrated. We had been a part of the intercession that week in Cuba that helped influence Castro's decision. It was then that we knew the reason we had been called to "stand in the gap" for the precious people of Cuba.

Since the day of that great declaration we have been invited to come to Cuba with Campus Crusade, the Jesus Film Project and Walk Through The Bible to teach Cuban educators in large convocations across the island. One day, perhaps, we might be able to go there to be a part of another great miracle. When that happens we will tell our dear Cuban brothers and sisters the story of our first visit.

Section III

Merry Mission Stories We Have Seen and Heard

30

"It Just Hit The Spot!"

"Pastor Jack! This Saturday night we have been invited to a live concert and banquet at a church down in St. Ann's Bay!" Pastor Moses was very excited to share this bit of news with us, since music and food are two of the most popular items in Jamaica. We were fairly new to the region at that time, and we wanted to learn more about the local culture and to get acquainted with other church members and leaders.

As we filed into the banquet and concert area that evening we were greeted with a large number of believers who were thrilled in anticipation of a great concert and a delicious meal. This banquet area was located on the second floor of the large church building. Pastor Moses was especially excited to tell us that they were serving one of his favorite dishes that evening. He felt that we would like it also. The name of the soup was "Mannish Water." This is the *patois* (local dialect) expression for "Man Soup!" It sounded rather fascinating and I was eager to try it. I had no idea what awaited my taste buds.

We were foreign missionaries and were treated with special courtesy that evening. We were some of the first guests to be served Mannish Water. I was challenged by what I saw, smelled and tasted! The soup was very spicy and greasy. The first sip convinced me that I was not "mannish" enough to consume that Jamaican delicacy. I looked at the soup again and noticed that it seemed to stare back at me! Then, I remembered that this was goat soup and it had goat parts floating around. I knew that I could never eat or swallow eyeballs and other sinister-looking pieces of a goat's anatomy. What was I to do? I did not want to hurt anyone's feelings. This was a favorite dish of the region and they would all want to know how well I enjoyed it. I was desperate for a solution. Then...I had an idea that could work. I whispered to Winona, above the sounds of the loud concert music, and said, "Mama-san, look out this window to my right!" She agreed. Then, I said, "Just remember that out that window is The Spot!" She looked at me in wonderment and asked, "What?"

"Don't worry, Winona, just remember what I said. That is The Spot!" She shrugged her shoulders and looked back to the stage where the concert was in full swing. The gospel music in Jamaica is played very loud with lots of motions of joy. Then, the song ended and everyone stood up to applaud the performers on the stage. I quickly dashed my soup out the window followed by a pretentious gesture that I was licking my spoon with gusto.

In a few minutes there was a break in the concert and several people came to our table to see how we were enjoying the concert and the banquet, especially the "Mannish Water." "Pastor Jack," they inquired, "How did you enjoy the Mannish Water?" I smiled as I responded truthfully, "It just hit The Spot!"

31

The Night We Loaded Marijuana in Jamaica

Albert Estes is our son-in-law. He is a very dedicated Christian and loves mission trips. Albert is a wonderful singer and musician and everyone loves his talents. Albert had come to Jamaica with a youth group to help us with Daily Vacation Bible Schools and other forms of ministry.

On this particular evening we were sleeping in a church named Gayle Church of Christ. There were a large number of teen boys and girls and they were all very tired after a day of work, worship and a swim in the local river. The evening service had lasted until after 10 o'clock and it was now approaching midnight and we finally got everyone settled down for a few hours of sleep, hopefully, before the early morning goats and roosters would begin their serenading. It was around 2:00 a.m., I think, when we heard some very loud and obtrusive noises outside the church. We detected that someone was playing a radio very loudly. Albert and I jumped out of our sleeping bags to see if we could convince the celebrants to lower the sound so that the American teens could get some sleep. Albert and I opened the side door of the church and stepped outside where we found a group of men loading a vehicle to the sound of Jamaican jazz. We stepped up to the vehicle and courteously asked if we could help them with the loading so that they would soon be on their way and we could get back to sleep.

After a few minutes of loading sacks of unknown leafy materials we noticed that these men were watching these two white American missionaries with an admixture of astonishment and disbelief. We had no idea why they kept looking at us that way. Then, we discovered why! We recognized, finally, what we were loading into their vehicle. It was *ganja!* That is the name of marijuana in Jamaica and we were collaborating with drug dealers. If we had been caught that night we would have been arrested with the other criminals. We both had a little trouble sleeping the rest of that night. We both, I'm sure, prayed a version of a famous prayer that night: "Forgive us! We didn't know what we were doing!"

32

I Nearly Died in the Jungle!

The festivals were coming to town and we knew that the streets and public square would be filled with thousands of "Mardi Gras" forms of celebration. This bustling community was located in the tropical hills of Bolivia. There would be an entire weekend of alcohol binges, cocaine flowing freely and other forms of carousing. This particular celebration would be highlighted by parades of Indian tribes dressed like "demons" and they would be allowed to enter the Catholic cathedral for a blessing before they began their pagan celebrations. We had seen these festivities before and felt that it would be wise to take our young men of the Evangelical Church out of the community for a couple of days.

We announced to a number of the teenage boys plus Dario Nuñez, one of our adult leaders, that we would be camping out along the river for part of the weekend. This river lay some 2,000 feet below the town of Coroico and it meandered through some dense forests and other beautiful sights.

We made the trek to the river in the mid-afternoon and I was advised by the young men that my job was to watch the bananas while they went in search of other fruits and food for our supper. These particular bananas could be boiled or fried and were considered a delicacy in that area. I was to guard a large quantity of these foodstuffs. I felt that my job was a cinch so I planned to sit under a shade tree alongside the river and relax. Wrong! Within a few minutes after our young men left the encampment I heard some very strange noises that seemed to be getting closer and closer. I look in astonishment to see a herd of wild hogs running toward me. They looked as if they were hungry. I made an instantaneous decision. I climbed the first available tree. I could not believe my eyes!

The wild hogs were not chasing me, but rather the bananas. I watched from the top of a tree as they enjoyed a banquet. They ate those bananas as if they were starving and made all kinds of sounds to show their appreciation. I clung to my tree. Soon the bananas were all gone and so were the pigs. Not one of them expressed gratitude for their free buffet.

I was reluctant to climb down since I was not sure what those greedy hogs might do to a scared white missionary. I just sat in the tree until I heard the voices of our youth group returning to the camp to prepare supper. They were very unhappy with the pigs and me for the disappearance of the main course for their evening meal. I slid to the ground and explained that I had no options since those pigs were, in my opinion, cannibalistic. The teens only laughed at me.

After supper we were placing our bedding materials around the campfire and were looking forward to a beautiful, quiet, restful evening. The teens finally convinced me, slightly, that hogs were not that dangerous. As we were making our beds, using leaves and other local fibers, we were startled by the appearance of one of the local natives. He was rather excited and told us in a very serious tone that, "today, I killed a boa in this area! It has a mate and he is very angry! You cannot sleep here tonight as the snake will probably try to take vengeance against you!" By this time I had my gear and was ready to follow the local Indian native.

He invited all of us to spend the night with his family that was housed in a small adobe hut covered with palm and bamboo. There was only one room and I was given the bed while the rest of the room was packed with his family and young men who would be sleeping on the floor. The small house was cramped and hot. There were no windows or doors that could be opened at night. I was not sure that I could ever get to sleep that night as I thought about wild boars and angry boas. Finally, I felt a cool breeze fanning my face and I was so happy that I, now, would be able to get some sleep. Then…it dawned on me that the breeze could not be for real. The temperatures outside and in were hot and all the windows and doors were closed. Something was wrong! I called for one of our young men named

Herman and asked him to please light a candle and bring it to my bed. Herman lighted the candle and I could not believe what I saw!

There in the semi-darkness was a large vampire bat and it was fanning my face. I was told later that they do this to animals and people to lull them to sleep, and, then suck the blood from veins or arteries. This one had been hovering near my neck. Herman was able to evict the blood-thirsty vampire from the room and then blew out the candle after another series of "Buenas Noches!" (Good Night!) I had some weird thoughts running through my mind.

Which is the most dangerous? Would it be a band of starving hogs; an angry boa constrictor; or, perhaps a thirsty vampire bat? I tossed and turned a bit that night.

A few years later we started a Youth Camp at Eagle Creek Evangelical Friends, with the help of Barry and Wanda Faucett and others, and we decided to name the camp after the Spanish name of that first camp down in Bolivia. And, this summer there will be a lot of children and youth who will attend the English version of that first jungle camp along a pig, snake and bat infested jungle. It is now sponsored by Church of Praise in Eagletown, Indiana, and is named "Camp Amigos!"

33

She Nearly Killed Me!

I had been invited to preach a revival campaign at a Nazarene Church near Rockville, Indiana, by my father-in-law Rev. Thomas Moody. The first night that I arrived at the church I was met in the foyer by two or three ladies. One of them greeted me by saying, "Pastor Terry, I have heard about you from our minister and I am so glad to meet you!" That welcome sounded very nice, but I had no idea what was to follow.

The lady who gave me that greeting was named Mrs. Farnsworth and she was so friendly, and also very large. After the warm greeting she stretched out her hand and took a step in my direction. At that moment she tripped over the carpet on the floor and lost her balance. She actually ran into my arms. I did my best to catch her and help her regain her balance. I had no idea of the momentum that Mrs. Farnsworth carried. As I caught her in my arms we both raced backwards in the church foyer and crashed against the wall. The building shook, if I remember correctly. Our precious sister carried more impact than anyone I had ever met prior to that meeting.

After the crash we both slid to the floor of the foyer and Sister Farnsworth landed on top of me. At first I was shocked, then embarrassed. Those feelings were followed by a weightier question: How am I going to get up? My new friend was unable to pick herself up. I think that she weighed over 350 pounds. I was having a few problems breathing, if I remember correctly. Silly questions fluttered in my mind, I'm sure. I probably thought, "If I don't survive, will the newspapers carry a column in the obituary column such as: Evangelist Dies of Overweight!" Oh no!

But I was saved by a couple of ushers who rescued me from my close friend. After I brushed off my suit, straightened my hair and other things that were in disarray, I think that I said to the very embarrassed Mrs. Farnsworth, "It was so nice to meet you!" I'll never forget that meeting.

34

The Night I Became a Terrorist!

We were sleeping in a church down in Jamaica. We had a youth team from Indiana and they were doing special programs of Daily Vacation Bible Schools for children plus music, skits and other ministries. On this particular night it began to rain. On this tropical island the rains sometime last for days. On this particular night everyone was very tired and was sleeping soundly as the rain beat a rhythm on the tin roof. The beds consisted of inflated air mattresses. Some nights the sleeping was interrupted by the snoring of teenagers and leaders, goats, roosters and other nuisances. The rain drowned out most of those noises. I suddenly encountered another problem! What could I do?

There was no bathroom in this church, which was located in a place called Gayle, Jamaica. I waited, hoping that the rain would subside for a moment so that I could escape the building and try to find the little outhouse behind the building in the pitch black night. The rain was now coming down in sheets. What could I do? I slipped to the side door and opened it partially and peeked outside. There was no chance of making it to the outhouse without being completely doused in the torrential downfall. Then, I had a survival thought! Everyone is asleep! Why not create a bathroom right there in the doorway? No one will ever know or care!

That was a dreadful error of judgment!

After I closed the two side doors that provided me an escape hatch I slithered silently back to my assigned pew where a nicely inflated air mattress awaited me. I anticipated a joyful night of sleep as the tropical rains sounded like soothing music. Then, I heard a shrill whisper, "Jack is that you?" It was Sonya (Dennis) Evans, a young member of our Mission Team. "Yes," I replied! Then I listened to the voices of Sonya and another girl friend saying, "We woke up and saw this figure standing in the doorway! We were so frightened. We began to pray because this man was already in the doorway and was coming inside!" The voices carried an admixture of fear and relief. "We are so relieved to know that it is you," they whispered above the rainfall. I was relieved also, until we arrived back in Indiana and the girls shared that "intruder story" with various congregations. I wish I had gone to the outhouse!

35

The Night They Tried to Steal
Our New Dodge Power Wagon

The year was 1954 and Winona and I had recently moved to Arica, Chile, which is located near the Pacific Ocean and on the edge of the driest desert in the world, the Atacamba. Today, this is a free port that serves Chile, Peru and Bolivia.

Our mission group, Youth for Christ, had provided us with a new Dodge Power Wagon which had the ability to navigate the dry, deep sand of the desert. In fact, we drove places where no other vehicles had ever driven. On one particular night following an evangelistic service out in the Atacamba, we lost our way returning to Arica and wound up inside Peru. We were totally unaware that we had crossed their border until we were suddenly surrounded by armed border guards. We were in serious difficulties until we found the correct visas. After a few moments of explaining, apologizing and paying a nice "tip," we were given our freedom and instructions on how to find the Chilean border.

At this point in time Winona was six months pregnant with our un-born son, Stephen. One night she awakened me around 2:00 or 3:00 a.m. with a loud whisper. "Jack," she said, "I just woke up and saw someone breaking into our truck. They are trying to steal it!" Wow! What could I do? We were new in the country and I did not speak more than a few words in Spanish. Should I wake up the other two male missionaries in the house? Missionaries Carlyle McFarland and Boyd Skinner and their families shared the same little house with us. Looking back on that moment I realize that I should have done that. But, instead I decided to run outside the house and apprehend the thief in the night.

I quickly opened the back door to the little mission house and raced toward the burglar. He was already inside the vehicle when I grabbed him, I think. He was startled and began to speak in a frightened Chilean accent. I had no idea what he was saying. I realized that although I had captured the truck thief I did not know what to do with him. All that I could remember in Spanish that might be appropriate was, "Que Paso?" (What happened?) I asked him this question two or three times and each time he gave me several eloquent explanations. I did not understand one word! Then, I thought of a plan. Perhaps I needed to teach him a nice little lesson.

I grabbed the scared thief by his right arm and began to escort him away from the scene. I never dreamed that, perhaps, we should have called the police. As I tugged his arm we began to walk faster and faster down the street. Then we began to trot. Neither of us knew where this little marathon would lead. Soon we were cantering, huffing and puffing. Just as we were getting close to the speed limit the Chilean thief lost his balance and tripped. He fell down onto the street and rolled through the sand that had blown in from the desert.

I could not think of anything to say to my frightened, exhausted race mate so I dusted off my hands and went back to Winona's bedroom. "What happened?" she asked. I couldn't give a logical explanation so we just went back to bed. I don't know how the Dodge Power Wagon thief rationalized that night. I imagine that he thought something like this: "Those *gringo* Americans are *loco!*" Well, at any rate, no one ever tried to steal our truck again.

36

I Talked with a Cannibal!

While doing missionary work in the Yungas of Bolivia in the 1950s we were so blessed to have met so many different kinds of people. This location was in the tropical mountains not too far from the dense forests and rivers of the jungle territories. Many of the local residents of the Yungas area were descendants of the Aymara Indian tribes. These indigenous tribes were pre-Inca and still spoke the ancient dialect of their forefathers. There were also a few black people whose forefathers had been brought to South America as slaves from Africa. One of the most interesting groups of people was a group of Jews who had been offered asylum during the time of the Holocaust. Of course, there were many who were descendants of the Spanish conquistadors who reigned in Bolivia in the 16th Century. One of the most intriguing classes of people was the cannibal descendants. On one particular evening I was fortunate to meet one of their members.

I cannot remember his name, but I will always remember that he was a born-again Christian and appeared to be very intelligent. It was exciting to talk with him about his former tribal customs and how he came to know Christ as his Savior. After a long discussion I had just about run out of questions. But, I had one question that I could not avoid. I knew that it was, most likely, inappropriate, but nevertheless I had to know. The question was, "Have you ever eaten another human being?"

I asked him that dastardly question and waited for his response. He did not hesitate to answer, "Yes!" Then, I asked one more question that still in my opinion today was a stupid one: "Which part did you like best?" Oh no! He looked at me and answered: "The hand!"

As he left the mission house that evening my mind was filled with an admixture of feelings. There was joy in my heart that this man had been saved and delivered from his tribal and demonic obsessions. There was also a feeling of relief that I had not met him before that miracle. In fact, I gave him my hand as he departed, although I think that I counted my fingers afterwards just to be sure!

37

The Day the Pope Gave Me a Blessing in the Vatican

In that particular summer I had worked in my spare time with an insurance company. I was the pastor of a church in Hamilton County and I was teaching in the Westfield Middle School. One of the bonuses for the insurance project was a free trip to Rome on a chartered airplane. That was a powerful incentive for me since I enjoy travels. I was given two free trips that summer, but Winona declined the journey and I made the crusade alone.

We were given a number of special visits to places such as the Roman Coliseum, the catacombs and many other highlights of that ancient city. Then we were told that we had a private audience with the Pope. We were impressed, but were not sure what we would see or hear from Pope Paul. We were all excited about his rather "evangelical remarks" as he declared, "Today's Christians have a historical relationship with Christ, but we all need a contemporary Christ who is with us here and now!" That was great, but we were not sure if those remarks were for the American tourists or if he preached that message universally. The next statement really caught my attention.

Pope Paul said, "I will bless any objects that you have brought here today. Please hold the item that you want blessed in your hand and extend your arm in my direction!" I was perplexed about what might be appropriate for such a papal blessing. Some of the tour group held out small icons, crosses and other things. I searched my pockets and could find nothing that needed a special blessing or that I should extend toward the leader of the Catholic world. Then, I realized that I had an object in my pocket that desperately needed a blessing. I fished it out of my pocket and pointed it toward the pope. I am not sure that the blessing took effect that day, however. You see, it was my billfold that really needed a blessing back in those days. Some of the tour group felt that my icon was, most likely, inappropriate!

38

Our Kids Robbed a Village!

In 1958 we lived in a friendly town in Bolivia named Coroico. In the first months of our ministry there, in 1956, we had faced persecution from a number of sources. Our church had not been able to open to the streets for more than two years prior to our going there. There had been episodes of stone throwing and dragging believers behind horses, and the most violent had been the public whipping of our pastor, Lorenzo Palomino, in the police station. But, God had worked several miracles and we were able to do our missionary work in complete safety and with the blessing of the entire community.

I had been named the Coroner of the city, plus they had given us a position as a teacher of English in the public school system. We also operated a free clinic that offered medications to the public. The ministries were flourishing and we were experiencing so many miracles in conversions, athletic programs and other activities. Then, one day we heard a commotion on our street.

Our Mission was located only one block from the main square of this bustling town. Alongside most of the streets leading to the town square were dozens of outdoor shops and other markets that sold many kinds of fruits and vegetables, and some household goods. On this particular day our three kids, Debby, Stephen and Marcia, all under six years of age, had decided to go shopping. They had seen their mother, Winona, and Ventura Choqenapi, a young Indian girl who lived with us, go shopping every week, and now they felt that it was their turn. They had not been aware that money was required so they were helping themselves to anything that looked delicious or attractive to their young appetites.

We were appalled, but the community was celebrating the occasion! They were applauding, laughing and cheering as our three children hijacked the town. By the time we discovered the great robbery their little baskets were full and their faces were flushed with victory. "We've been shopping!" they declared triumphantly in Spanish.

We had no options except to enter into the spirit of peace and good will; however, as soon as possible we made attempts to make restitution to the shopkeepers, who insisted on our keeping the goods. In fact, it was heartwarming to hear expressions such as "De nada! No importa! Que hermoso!" (You are welcome! Don't worry! How beautiful!) We still laugh about that special day when the missionary children robbed a village!

39

Cary Woodward's Duel
with an Angry Goat

Cary Woodward is one of my heroes. I first came to know him back in the 1980s when he was the director of an insurance company. Since that time we have had so many great church and mission experiences. Cary gave his heart totally to the Lord and helped us in so many ways while we were pastors at Christ Community Church. Another of my heroes, Buddy Clark, was so instrumental in helping Cary find a job with the Hamilton County Weights and Measures Department and today you will see Cary's name on every gas pump in Hamilton and Boone counties.

Cary has made more than one mission trip to Jamaica, where he helped us with a variety of building projects and other work. On one of those trips he experienced a dangerous encounter with an angry goat.

We were working that day at a place called Gayle, Jamaica, which is located about 35 miles east of the Caribbean port city of Ocho Rios. The entire team had been working very hard on some carpentry, Daily Vacation Bible School sessions and a lot more. The weather was hot. The indoor bathroom facilities did not exist at Gayle. There was one small, smelly and slightly sloppy outhouse that was located behind the church and quite near a small cemetery. Since there was no running water it did not take long for the entire toilet to become very damp and utterly revolting. Brother Cary Woodward was in dire need of a restroom, but elected to find another facility. He decided to test the small forest of lush vegetation located not far from the church. This is his version of "Cary Woodward's confrontation with a hostile billy goat":

I was in dire need of some biological relief and elected to by-pass the outdoor "privy" and to find a tropical setting amidst the trees, bushes and flowers located on that fairly remote hillside. I made sure that there were no other human beings in the area and then began to concentrate on my immediate needs. I had just become comfortable when I was startled to discover that I was not alone. I felt a small sensation of uneasiness as I looked directly in the eyes of a hostile billy goat!

I realized that I had invaded his turf and that he was unhappy with my presence. Perhaps he had never seen another white man in my position. What could I do? I had no other choices. I couldn't wait any longer. I looked that angry goat right in the eyes and I made this statement: "Mr. Goat, if you are going to make your move, you had better do it quickly, because I am going to make mine!"

40

"It Smells Like Pancakes!"

"Jack, will you check my oil?" I awakened from my sleep to hear Winona asking me to check her auto before she left for work at an Indianapolis Nursing Home operated by our son-in-law, Albert Estes. She had to leave about an hour earlier to work than I did. I wiped the sleep out of my eyes and felt my way to the garage where our Oldsmobile was parked. I opened the hood and discovered that the car was more than two quarts low. I wasn't sure if I had any oil so I began to look on the shelves, but found nothing. So, I opened the trunk of Winona's vehicle and saw a number of cans that had all the appearance of oil. What else could it be?

I opened one of the "oil cans" and it had all the appearance of motor oil. So, I opened the cans and poured them into the engine. I felt good that I could help Winona with her little problem as she thanked me for my mechanical skills, and then she drove to Glendale. I still had nearly an hour before I would have to leave for my teaching job at the Westfield Middle School. I had time for a nice hot cup of coffee before my day began.

I still remember that fateful telephone call that I received later that afternoon from Winona. "Jack, the car stopped on Highway 31 near a filling station and I can't get it started," she said in an ominous tone. "Do you have any idea what might have happened?" I asked as I prepared to drive down to the stalled vehicle. "No!" she answered, "but it smells like pancakes!"

My mind began to race feverishly as I tried to understand what might have happened. Then...a horrible thought entered my mind.

I remembered that a friend down in Cadiz, Indiana, where we had served a church a few months earlier, had given us some maple syrup from his little cannery. In fact, he had all of the instruments to extract the sap from the tree and boil the maple syrup. He had canned several quarts for us in new motor oil cans. Oh no!

The car had to be towed to the repair shop and the motor had to be overhauled. The cost was horrendous. The head mechanic spoke to me confidentially and said, "Mr. Terry, I think someone sabotaged your car and put some syrup in the engine. You might want to report this to the police!"

I will always remember the day that someone mistakenly put two quarts of maple syrup in Winona's car and that "it smelled like pancakes!" I wonder who might have "sabotaged" her car?

41

The Blonde Lady in the Tavern

"Pastor Terry, will you come to our house and pray for my husband?" The lady's voice sounded very distraught so I agreed to come right away to see if I could be of help to that family.

This particular lady was a faithful believer and attended the services regularly. Her husband, I was told, was not a believer. In fact, he was rather indiscreet in his behavior and drinking habits. I prayed as I drove to Carmel to try to restore this family. As I drove up to the lovely home I realized that "we had a problem." "My husband just left the house when he heard that you were coming to pray for him," the nice lady explained. "He has gone down to the tavern on Main Street in Carmel," she said. "I think we should go down there and talk with him," she volunteered. I was not so sure.

We drove down to the well known tavern and I felt very uncomfortable. This lady was an attractive blonde female and I did not want to be seen driving toward a tavern with her seated beside me. What could I do? We arrived at the tavern and faced another dilemma. "Let's go inside and talk with him," the lovely blonde lady suggested. Oh no! How can I walk into a tavern with a blonde on my arm? People will suspect something and talk! But, what could I do? I prayed a prayer of protection and entered that dimly lit tavern with a blonde lady some twenty years younger than I was. I prayed desperately.

As we walked into the pub that evening; her husband saw us coming. He jumped up from the table and raced outside the back door and escaped into his car. By this time I was feeling a bit indignant. If I had paid this price of humiliation and embarrassment to talk to this man I was not about to let him escape! So, we walked swiftly out to my car and drove back to their home. When we arrived at the house the lady searched for her husband and discovered that he had jumped into bed and covered up his head. She called me from the upstairs bedroom and invited me to come and "pray with her husband." I will never forget that scene.

Something had happened to me during that episode of going to the tavern and chasing an elusive, half-drunk spouse. I felt some righteous indignation! Without thinking of the consequences I jumped into bed with the man and uncovered him. He was fully dressed and in a state of bewilderment. He could run no more. He surrendered. And, so there, that night in a lovely Carmel bedroom, we had a fervent prayer meeting. The setting might have seemed a little out of place, but our great God loves all of us. He loved that precious couple that night and brought a spirit of repentance and reconciliation. I consider it a miracle. I hope that I never have to do evangelism in quite that same way again.

42

Earth's Bloodiest Road

National Geographic magazine has labeled the road from La Paz to Coroico, Bolivia, the most dangerous road in the world. Recently a special TV program featured that road that Winona and I once knew very well. In fact, it was the only road available from the tropical mountains of North Yungas to La Paz, the highest capital city in the world. We were compelled to drive on this "bloody road" frequently.

The "Bloody Road" is called that because of the nature and location of this highway, which curves like a serpent along the high mountains of the Andes down to the beautiful and fruitful tropics of Bolivia. The road begins at the edge of the high plains of Bolivia, where many descendants of the Inca and Aymara Indians still live today. These plains are more than 10,000 feet above sea level. The road was carved out of the sides of the mountains by prisoners of war from Paraguay.

Most of the road is barely wide enough for one vehicle. Much of the traffic consists of trucks carrying coffee, fruit and vegetables from the verdant Yungas to the marketplaces of La Paz. The road rises higher than clouds and is not wide enough for traffic to pass. One of the vehicles must back up, most of the time, to a designated passing spot. This can be very hazardous when traffic is heavy and the weather is foggy and wet.

Most of the time the drivers on this "Death Road" must keep their eyes focused on the road ahead plus blowing their horns to alert oncoming traffic. Many times this is not enough and collisions happen. In most cases these accidents are fatal because of the thousands of feet that the vehicles will fall down to the valley below. When I served as Coroner of the village of Coroico, located at the end of the

123

"Bloodiest Road in the World," the officials would sometimes notify me to come and examine the bodies of the dead or to treat any survivors. Those were gruesome scenes.

On one occasion, Winona and I needed to travel to La Paz, in our ancient Jeep, for some supplies and to have the brakes repaired. The brakes had gone out on the 1946 yellow Jeep and there were no repair shops down where we lived. So, we decided to drive the eighty-plus miles to La Paz without brakes. We knew that this would be terribly hazardous, but we had an idea that might work! We would just rely on prayer and the emergency brakes to get us through. But, how could I focus on the roads and, at the same time, pull the emergency brake at the many curves where we would be required to stop instantly? Then, we had a brilliant idea! We would ask Dario Nuñez, our youth leader and the son-in-law of the mayor of Coroico, to be our "living emergency brakes."

So, as we began that exciting adventure, we practiced our strategies of "stopping on a dime" by yelling "stop!" (*pare!* in Spanish). The trick was that Dario had to sit on my left side as we drove that more-than-four-hour ordeal. There was not enough room for both of us to sit behind the wheel, so parts of our dear brother Dario were hanging over the side of the Jeep. Of course, we could not close the left door, either. So, after prayer and other preparations we began an upwards journey from around 3,000 feet altitude in Coroico to more than 11,000 feet in La Paz. Of course, Winona was seated on my right side and she could peek out the window and look directly down through the clouds to see the tiny ribbon of a river that snaked its way from the high plains of the Andes down to the tributaries of the mighty Amazon.

Winona would have her hands full that day, also. She had to help me watch the narrow, bloody road ahead plus babysit our three children, Deborah, Marcia and young Stephen. If the children were not watched carefully, they tended to hang over the sides or sometimes play frisky games as we traveled. Once, Stephen ran from the front seat of the little yellow Jeep to the back curtain and tumbled to the ground. Winona had her hands full that day.

Dario and I had a rather uneventful day as we maneuvered the jeep over that dangerous road. After several episodes of yelling "Pare!" we became a team of pilot and copilot. Sometimes there were only a matter of inches, it seemed, between our front bumper and the oncoming vehicle that was screeching to a sudden halt. Here and there were marked grim reminders of where other vehicles had not survived. I remember that we prayed a lot, laughed a lot and yelled "Pare!" Often times other professional truck drivers looked at us, I think, as if we were slightly crazy. Finally, we reached the plateau of the high plains of the Department of La Paz and drove merrily into the city. We had survived! We rejoiced that day as we were reminded of God's protection and love for a yellow Jeep full of missionaries. I think that our guardian angels might have asked for a few days vacation after that "Bloodiest Road" nightmare.

43

"Don't Play Marbles in the House!"

Nicholas was one of the first homeless children to move into our small orphanage in Golden Grove, Jamaica. Nicholas was about five years old at that time and had lost his mother a few months prior to that time. Everyone called this little boy "Nick." He moved into the orphanage with two sisters and three brothers. He was a very shy young boy at that time and usually kept his fingers in his mouth. This was, in my opinion, a sign that Nick missed his mother very much and was subconsciously reverting back to the breast feeding days. Nick had another childhood problem, also. He loved to play with fire.

So many times I was told by his sisters and brothers that "Nicholas was playing with matches in the house!"

I warned and reprimanded little Nick many times. The problem got worse and it was apparent that we needed to take some serious measures. In my opinion this young man had almost become a pyromaniac. I called Nick to the backyard where we could talk in confidence. I was prepared to administer some severe consequences if this discussion did not produce some radical changes. Nicholas was very somber as I began to recall all the times he had been caught playing with matches, cigarette lighters and "strikers," as we call the handheld stove lighters in Jamaica.

"Nicholas, tell me where did this problem of playing with matches begin?" Nicholas looked at me fearfully for a moment and gave this response: "When I was little my brothers and I would play marbles in the house. One day a marble rolled under the bed and we couldn't find it. We began to strike matches to see if we could find that marble. The bed caught on fire and they had to drag me out the window.

126

The house burned down!"

I could hardly believe what I was hearing. I then asked Nicholas another question. "Nicholas, then what did you learn from that lesson?" Nick looked at me again and very seriously answered: "I learned that you should never play marbles in the house!"

44

"Why Did You Throw Your Bible at Me?"

I had just climbed up to the second floor of the mission house in Bolivia. I had attended the Bible Study and Prayer Meeting and the hour was growing late. Winona had not been able to attend that evening. When I entered the bedroom I found that she and the three children, Debby, Stephen and Marcia, were all asleep.

I tiptoed into the room so as not to wake them and I saw something that horrified me. There was a very large, poisonous scorpion crawling down the side of the wall and was heading in the direction of Winona's hair. I knew that those creatures were very dangerous and if it got into her hair it could be deadly. It was now only a few inches from her head and crawling straight toward Winona! I had no time to think. I grabbed the Bible that I was holding in my hand and flung it with full force toward the potential killer.

The loud sound of the Bible smashing into the wall awakened Winona and she sat up in bed and was completely startled. She looked down and saw the Bible on her pillow and she uttered a fairly loud protest of, "Jack, why did you throw your Bible at me?"

I pointed at the bloody smear of the scorpion on the wall just above her pillow. Winona looked and was so happy that she had been rescued. I was happy, also, that I had hit the target and was out of the doghouse.

That was one of the best shots I ever made.

45

An Escaped Killer in Winona's Bathroom

I had been away from the Mission Compound in Bolivia for several days and returned to hear this very exciting story. Winona related to me that one day after my departure the police came to her door. In fact, there was a group of them and they were heavily armed. Winona asked them why they had come, and they said, "Señora Terry, there is a dangerous escaped criminal here inside your mission. He escaped from our prison several miles down the river." Winona refused to believe the story, thinking that they were mistaken. "I am sure that he is not here, sir!" she replied.

"Señora Terry," the squad commander insisted, "We are sure that he is here. Do we have your permission to search for him?" After several attempts to get the officers to look elsewhere Winona agreed to allow them to look throughout the mission facilities. The search took some time and the police could not find their dangerous escapee. Then, one of the officers made an unusual discovery.

"Here he is!" The military policemen quickly handcuffed the prisoner and dragged him outside the compound to the street. "Señora Terry, we found this very dangerous escaped criminal. He was hiding in your outhouse!"

Winona thought it was an exciting and funny story, since she is fearless and knew that she has angels that watch over her.

46

"Please Tell Me Which Wife to Keep!"

I will call him Fernando since I cannot remember his actual name. He had recently been converted to Christ and knew that he must change several things in his lifestyle. Prior to becoming a believer, Fernando had, most likely, cultivated and chewed coca leaf (from which cocaine is made) and drank *chicha,* which is a homemade alcoholic beverage made from fermented grain. Another form of sin in that part of the world was that many men were accustomed to having more than one "wife." Fernando realized that to be a child of God, he would have to make these changes. He called me to help him decide!

I was totally out of my realm as Fernando asked me to help choose which lady he should marry. I did not know anything about the two women in his life so I innocently asked him to describe the character qualities in both of his former concubines. Here are some of the traits that he related to me.

"One of my *mujeres* (women) is a very good cook and housekeeper!" The other one has lots of *polleras* (skirts)!" In that post-Inca culture it is very fashionable for the ladies to wear several skirts at the same time. (These dresses are rather expensive and give the wife and her husband a feeling of success.)

After listening to the new Christian convert explain the top attributes of his former helpmates, I offered to do the wedding after he made the final choice. I was flabbergasted when I heard his choice. "I have chosen the lady with the most dresses!"

47

"Daddy! You Will Have to Fix That in the Morning!"

Chile, South America, was noted as one of the areas in the world that had the most earthquakes and tremors. It was a common experience to suddenly feel the strong vibrations pulsating through the community, and sometimes a powerful swaying that resulted in severe damage to homes. On one occasion an earthquake that occurred at sea a few miles away from our city, Arica, produced a tsunami and brought a large ship, "The Wateree," almost one quarter mile inland and deposited it in the Atacamba Desert.

On one occasion our little family was preparing for sleep inside the small church building where we lived for several months. The entire church suddenly began to shake and the force threw me and our little daughter, Deborah, on the floor. We sat there for a moment waiting to see what might happen next. Then, the tremors stopped and all was calm. Deborah, three years old, looked at me and said, "Daddy! You will have to fix that in the morning!"

48

"Huh-uh! I'm Not Dead!"

She was more than ninety years old when she gave her heart to Christ. I was so pleased to have been her pastor and friend. It seemed that we spent some time together each week sharing blessings and praying. Her health began to fail and the family decided to place Eve in the Carmel Nursing Home. I continued to visit her on a weekly basis. She kept her spirit of wit and sharpness of mind to the very end. One day I got a call from the administration that she had passed away.

I drove to Carmel with a sense of sadness, but also of gladness. We would miss our precious sister, but we knew that she was now in heaven and would be rejoicing in her new mind and body. When I arrived at the nursing home I was met by some of the directors, who told me the following story. "Eve died a while ago and we have called the family to tell them to come. We would like for you to break the news to her children that she died easily with no pain or problems." They escorted me to Eve's room, where she lay on her bed completely covered from head to foot. She had been examined and there were no vital signs.

I walked into Eve's room, where we had laughed, talked and prayed together many times in the past. I looked at the form of her body lying still under the covers. I began to pray that the Lord would help me to minister to the family when they arrived. In a few minutes her loved ones rushed into the room.

Some of the family was weeping openly. Others were asking me questions, such as "Did she die peacefully?" I began to tell them what the medical staff had told me about her quiet and peaceful home-going. I said, "She died very peacefully!" At that moment we were all shocked out of our shoes!

"Huh-uh! I'm not dead!" It was Eve! She was alive! We all ran to her bedside to uncover the frail, aged mother and grandmother. The family began to celebrate and rejoice that Mama and Grandma was alive! We called the staff and they came running. They could not believe their eyes! Eve was alive!

After a few moments I left the family to continue their celebration. No one could explain how the medical staff had not found any signs of life and had pronounced Eve dead. We were all mystified. It could only have been a miracle to help bring all the family closer to each other and Him. In a few days Sister Eve did make her final farewell and went to be with Jesus. The funeral was so precious because each of us knew in our hearts that Eve was still alive and well in heaven. I will never forget those exciting words she uttered that day in the Carmel Nursing Home: "Huh-uh! I'm not dead!"

49

I Found a Fortune Under Her Arm!

Following a few months of persecution in a tropical town located in the mountain country of Bolivia, we were offered several wonderful proposals by the local government. One invitation was to teach English and French in the government school and another was to become the Coroner. I was delighted to be able to teach in the Junior High and High School departments. That offered so many open doors for ministry in the months to come. I was not quite sure about the Coroner's job, although I had been trained in some medical technology with the Arkansas and Indiana State Boards of Health. I consented to both jobs.

One fateful day I received an urgent call from the local police to come to a specified building, where I would need to give some medical treatment to some victims of armed robbery. I collected my medical first-aid kit and moved quickly to the designated spot, where I found one or two corpses plus two others who were seriously wounded. One man had been shot in the neck and, to my surprise, when I probed into the wound with my forceps I found that the bullet had gone completely through the neck and no permanent damage had occurred. Following some antiseptic cleansing and injections of penicillin, the victim was released. The next patient was a different story.

What I saw was very hard to describe. The wounded lady, in her forties, weighed more than 250 pounds and had suffered several cuts and abrasions. The robbers suspected that she knew where the money was stashed and had beaten her about the head and she was unconscious. After checking her vital signs, I realized that she would, most likely, survive the incident, but would need a lot of treatments to stop the bleeding and cleanse a number of serious wounds. She did not move as I washed her wounds and administered injections for the infections. It was necessary to partially disrobe the very large Indian lady in order to swab and bandage all of the cuts on her upper torso. Then, I lifted her very large upper arm and discovered something that made me gasp in astonishment.

I could not believe what I saw when I looked under her very large armpits. She had stashed the family treasure under one armpit and it had not been discovered throughout the entire ordeal. When I casually counted the large bills I discovered that a small fortune had been hidden from the bandits. This was then kept for her until she regained consciousness. She was so happy that all of her family, except one, had survived the attacks and that they had not lost their family savings. In such cases we were free to counsel and pray with the patients. It is hard to remember all the details, but I sincerely hope that I advised her to find another vault to keep the family savings in.

50

Winona Nearly Got Drunk!

Winona was brought up in a very strict Quaker home, and the very thought of drinking alcohol in any form was totally forbidden. She had never even tasted wine, although she had been offered tiny cups of fermented *vino* in countries such as Israel, Italy, Chile, and so on. She always refused politely as she stated that "I have never tasted alcohol!" One night on a flight to Jamaica her "total abstinence vow" was severely tested.

We had been waiting for hours in the Miami airport for a plane to take us to Montego Bay, Jamaica, where Pastor Moses had been waiting for hours. There had been a series of cancellations and delays and now the hour was very late. Winona was feeling the discomfort of the muggy evening plus an overpowering thirst for something cold and refreshing. When we boarded a substitute flight on Meridian Airlines around midnight, she was elated when the airline hostess announced on the speakers that cold refreshments were available and they were free! Winona immediately ordered her favorite drink from Jamaica, one that is always available on Jamaican Airlines. She did not hesitate as she told the hostess what she wanted: "Champagne!"

Champagne Cola is a soft drink in Jamaica and is offered also on Air Jamaica. Winona had no idea that this word might have a different connotation on another Caribbean airline. Soon, the stewardess returned and handed Winona a tall glass of cold beverage. She was so thirsty that she gulped several swallows before she realized that she was tasting fire. She began to cough, sputter and wipe her mouth with a handful of napkins. "What is this?" she demanded. The apologetic stewardess took the rest of Winona's "Champagne Cola." Then, she asked my precious wife another fateful question: "Would you like something else, madam?"

By this time Winona had calmed down, although she had no idea why the cold Champagne Cola was so hot. She thought for a moment and then made her second request to the kind airline stewardess. "Just bring me some punch," she requested, while trying to understand the differences in the beverages on two allied airlines. Soon the eager-to-please stewardess returned to our seats and graciously handed Winona her cold punch. At last! Now, finally she would be able to quench that dry thirst. She had waited for this moment for hours. She took the cold glass and, again, began to gulp the icy punch. Oh no! Winona was repeating the same maneuvers as before. "Something is wrong with this punch!" she gasped. I took the half-empty glass and smelled the contents. I was appalled. This was not punch! This was Caribbean rum!

Finally we were able to find Winona a non-sinful drink and she calmed down for the rest of the flight into Montego Bay. I do my best not to smile at the innocence on her face when, even today, she declares,

"I have always been a *tee-totaler!*"

51

"Does He Talk to Those People?"

One day Winona told me that she was having a fairly large women's group at our parsonage-home that afternoon. She advised me to move into a small back room where I would have privacy and that she would bring me the phone if there were calls.

As I sat in the back room, I could hear the talking and laughter of this women's group. I also heard the telephone ring. I heard Winona say in a fairly loud voice, "Jack, Moses wants to talk to you!" I thought nothing of it since this Moses was our pastor friend calling from Jamaica.

Then, a few minutes later, amidst the sounds of the women's group, I heard the telephone ring again. This time Winona's voice declared, "Jack you have a call from Abraham!" She did not explain to the ladies that Moses and Abraham were our friends. Abraham was one of the guides who worked with us in Israel. When I gave the phone back to Winona the ladies were wearing puzzled looks, if I remember correctly.

Then, to top it all the phone rang a third time! This time it was Noah calling. Dr. Noah is a counselor friend from Carmel, Indiana, and he wanted to chat for a moment. This was too much. The ladies demanded an explanation. They insisted on knowing "if Jack talks with those famous men from the Bible." It was a great relief and laugh when they discovered that these were ordinary men with Bible names. For a moment, they thought I had some high connections.

Section IV

Some Missionary Tongue Twisters

We have seen and heard so many different languages around the world. In Jamaica we have to be able to speak *patois* and English, while in Haiti it is Creole and French. Down in Bolivia, in the early days, it was necessary to speak Aymara, a pre-Inca dialect, and Spanish. When we are in Russia and China we are confronted with other difficult language barriers and in India there are hundreds of dialects. Here are a few examples of how easy it is for missionaries to mess up the language while they are in the process of learning.

52

"Put It on Your Roof!"

During the late 1950s, Winona and I operated a small clinic in the tropical mountains of Bolivia. The medications were supplied primarily by donation from the USA and the UN Mission to Bolivia. I had met the Surgeon General of the UN through a "miracle meeting" and he offered to supply all of the antibiotics and tuberculosis injections that we could use. The very day that I met him I had been attending an Indian who had been bitten by a scorpion. He told me that he was going to die. I did not have any treatments for scorpion bites so I consulted with the famous Dr. Tichauer of the United Nations Mission. He said to me, "Yes, he will die of superstition and fear because he will stop eating and slowly die." He said to me, "Give him an injection of Vitamin B12 in his hip and tell him that he is going to get well." I did as I was told and, sure enough, the man believed that he was healed and he recovered instantly. That was a powerful example of the effects of superstition and fear.

I was able to treat many patients during the years that we lived in that village. It was such a joy to offer free life-saving medications plus Jesus Christ as their Lord and Savior. One day I gave a very silly prescription. I was trying to help a man who had an infection in his chest. The word in Spanish for chest is *pecho*. Instead of telling the patient that he should apply the remedy to his *pecho* I told him to put it on his *techo!* The word *techo* means "roof of your house." The poor man took the medication and went home. He came back in a few days to tell me a very humorous story. He said, "Pastor, I put the medication on my *techo* like you said and I really feel much better."

53

"I Love You!"

As we studied the Spanish language down in Chile, South America, back in 1954 we soon recognized that we were going make lots of mistakes. The local Chilean residents of the port city of Arica enjoyed hearing us trying to talk their language. They laughed along with us and would try to help us correct our mistakes. One day I made a serious language "gaffe." They thought it was funny when I called sweet potatoes "underwear," and one night when I caught a thief breaking in our Dodge Power Wagon I grabbed him and could only think of one sentence in Spanish: "Que Paso?" (What happened?) Duh!

I thought that it would be fun to go to the local tea shop to get acquainted with the people and to practice my Spanish. I decided to order a cup of hot tea, a favorite in that part of the world. I knew quite well the word for tea, which is *te*. The word for "desire or want" is *quiero*. So, to say "I want tea," you must say, "*Quiero te!*" When I made my request to the young Chilean waitress I made a horrible mistake!

If you wish to say, "I love you," in Spanish you may say, "*Te quiero!*" That is exactly backwards than asking for tea! So, when the pretty little waitress asked me what I wanted to order all of the people in the restaurant turned to see what the young, white Americano would order. I looked at the menu for a moment then I directed my attention to the young lady and said with confidence: "*Te quiero Señorita!*" The entire restaurant burst forth with Latino laughter. Instead of asking for tea I had said, "I love you, Señorita!" Oh no!

54

Go, and Compel Them to Come in!"

We were holding special Saturday night evangelistic services in the Codpa Valley of northern Chile. This valley is an oasis in the driest desert in the world, the Atacamba, where it may only rain once every 30 years. This is due to the cold current (El Niño) that flows from Antarctica along the coast of Chile and prevents evaporation and precipitation. The Codpa Valley is watered by the melting snows that descend from high up in the Andes Mountains. The Codpa Valley is known for its abundance of fruits, olives and vegetables. The inhabitants are also friendly, hardworking and open to the gospel.

On this particular Saturday night we had a nice audience inside the little sanctuary, while many others were watching through the open windows, doors and wide cracks in the bamboo structure. The preaching had been fervent and now it was time for the "Invitation" to be given for sinners to come forward to repent and receive Christ into their hearts. The American missionary gave a very powerful challenge to all the believers, although he did not realize that he was using an American "idiom." He urged the believers to "go out and compel them to come in!" That meant, that by our testimony, prayers and influence we could have a positive effect on the "outsiders." The Christian brothers inside the church took the challenge literally and raced outside and began dragging people inside the church. For several minutes there was a turmoil as scuffling believers came dragging the resistant sinners to the altars. A small dust storm filled the inside of the sanctuary, as the floors were pure desert sand. There were a few muffled protests that were soon stifled as those zealous Chilean brothers wrestled their captives to the sand in front of the altars and began to pray with them.

The American missionaries were transfixed by this new form of evangelism. We had never seen that type of "rescuing the perishing" before. To everyone's relief and joy the "new converts" were smiling and seemed to be very happy that they had been invited to church that night.

55

"Put Your All on the Altar!"

In the USA we are so accustomed to using "idioms" and other colorful expressions of the English language. In other countries these phrases, such as "He was fit to be tied"; "I'm tied up tonight"; "It will knock your socks off," and so on, are very difficult to translate.

On one occasion, while preaching in Bolivia, the missionary challenged his audience to "put their all on the altar." He was so surprised to see one of the faithful believers, a rather elderly man, go forward to the altar and climb up on top and squat like a hen laying an egg. I think that he was glad that the entire audience didn't try that.

56

Yellow-Blue-Bus!

Pastor Larry Renihan and I were so blessed to have worked in Russia with Walk through the Bible, the Jesus Film Project and Campus Crusade. During those training programs we were able to instruct the Russian teachers and administrators with a special curriculum that was Bible based. I enjoyed learning and practicing the Russian language with so many of those precious instructors and our university student interpreters.

All of us were blessed to have been able to build relationships with those former Soviet Union faculty members and to see many of them come to Christ during our convocations. One of our favorite ways of building these connections was to learn some of their language and to spend time with them after the teaching session. Many times we would be invited to their homes for dinner or to accompany a group of them to visit a tourist site in their community.

Our American faculty team usually consisted of more than forty teachers from all over America. On one occasion we had a teacher from the state of Georgia, USA. He had a keen desire to communicate with his assigned group of Russian teachers. One of the favorite expressions in the Russian language is: "We love you!" I have found that to be such a door-opener in that part of the world. Our friend from Georgia learned the expression and couldn't wait to try it on his group of ten female teachers. The only problem is that he failed to take into account his deep southern drawl. The way to say, "We love you," is *ya-la-blu-vas!* (Of course the Russian language is normally written in Greek-style letters.)

The next day our friendly southern-USA teacher greeted his class members with that lovely phrase. In fact he used it several times throughout the day. Many times that week he reminded these teachers of his love for them. They would smile, of course, with a tiny bit of puzzlement. You see, they did not understand his pronunciation, nor did his interpreters. These young university translators understood English quite well. They did, however, speak English with a British accent. When they heard the repetition of *yalabluvas,* they thought he was speaking in English. They came to us and asked: "Why does that American teacher from Georgia keep telling us about 'yellow blue buses'?"

57

I Mistranslated the Message at Westfield Middle School

"Mr. Terry, will you interpret a message for me? We have a group of Mexican kids here in the Middle School that have head lice and that could infect the whole school." This was the request presented to me by our very nice, but strict, school nurse. I agreed to help her with this rather drab message.

There were around ten Mexican moms that had been invited to this special meeting. They looked rather apprehensively at me as I entered the room. Until that moment they had not been able to communicate with the school nurse.

"I want you to know," the serious-toned message began, "that we have strict regulations here in our school regarding infectious diseases." I realized that we had not greeted the mothers that afternoon so I translated the bad news like this: "We are very happy to have your children in our school and we wish to give you a warm welcome." The room lit up with smiles. My nurse-friend looked at me with a bit of curiosity.

The no-nonsense message continued.

"I have discovered that your children have head lice and that is prohibited in this school!" I did not know how to break that bit of news in an open meeting. I said, "We hope that you will enjoy our community and school." The Latin-American smiles increased. The nurse frowned as she continued her warnings. Then, the meeting was dismissed and our nurse left the room. I quickly called all of the mothers into a huddle and whispered the true translation. "Our nurse has discovered head lice on your children and she wishes you to begin this prescribed remedy."

Each Mexican mom gave me assurance that they would cooperate.

147

Everyone was happy that day and I had survived what could have been a "revolution."

Section V
Spiritual Warfare
Around the World

The knowledge of Spiritual Warfare is the most important and vital training for ministry. So many pastors, evangelists and missionaries are totally untrained and unprepared for the battle of reaching and teaching the lost. St. Paul reminds us that "our struggle is not against flesh and blood, but against the rulers, against the authorities, against the powers of this dark world and against the spiritual forces of evil in the heavenly realms" (Ephesians 6:12). So many pastors in America and around the world have suffered major attacks and defeats because they were unprepared for battle. Jesus began His ministry with an attack from Satan in the wilderness. It was in that battle that the Lord showed us that we overcome by the blood of the Lamb and the Word of Testimony (the Bible)! (Revelation 12:11)

In our ministries in America and around the world we have found that we must put on the whole armor of God and take the shield of faith and the sword of the Spirit (the Word of God) and do warfare against the world, the flesh and the devil.

Here is a sample prayer that has rescued us and enabled us to be "more than conquerors."

Warfare Prayer: "Heavenly Father, I bow in worship and praise before you. I cover myself with the blood of the Lord Jesus Christ as my protection. I surrender myself completely and unreservedly in every area of my life to You! I take a stand against all the workings of Satan that would hinder me in my prayer life. I address myself only to the True and Living God and refuse any involvement of Satan in my prayer. Satan, I command you, in the name of the Lord Jesus Christ, to leave my presence with all your demons. I bring the blood of the Lord Jesus Christ between us and I pray in His Precious Holy Name!"

Here are a few instances of demonic attacks and how the Father delivered us from those attacks and gave us great victory.

58

House Heart Attacks

We had faced many forms of spiritual attacks after we opened the decaying, abandoned church building in Lamong, near Sheridan, Indiana. We had heard that the building had been closed due to a number of curses placed against that church over a period of many years. We knew that the Lord wanted us to reopen that building and began a new church named Christ Community Church. The first services were challenging and, on occasion, horrific!

We began worship services in Lamong in the fall of 1992. At first there were only a few people in attendance but we continued to ring the bell and open the doors. Little by little the audience grew in spite of the uncomfortable benches and "spiritual attacks." Several times the old furnace in the basement would begin to "belch smoke" that caused every person to run outside until the sanctuary could be cleared. We would just pray and believe that we were in the center of His will. Then, one day the Lord spoke to my heart and said that, "the property and building must be cleansed from the demons that had 'dwelt' on those premises for many years." As I prayed this is the message that I received.

The Lord seemed to say to me that I must "take the cross" from the front of the old sanctuary and drag it over every part of the property." That wooden cross weighed about 50 pounds, I think!

I took down the cross and began to drag it across the CCC properties. I'm sure that someone saw me and wondered what was going on. That "spiritual warfare" proved to be one of the major keys to the future success of Christ Community. Then, we felt led to have some of the members who believed in intercessory prayer to help us each Sunday by anointing the inside of the church with oil. This was one of the greatest keys to the future growth of that little, old, decaying building in Lamong. We were so blessed to have volunteers to come during the week and pray at the altars while others would pray in the office while the Word was being preached. Another great key was to have prayer warriors like Doug Beale and others to anoint the speaker after he had completed the sermon.

From those first infant stages of spiritual growth and warfare we saw many miracles. We were able to form prayer teams who were available to intercede for the church or for homes that were facing difficulties. The greatest miracles were the great number of new converts that were added to the church during those days. Here is one example of a home that was "demon possessed" and how a few simple, faith-believing Christians were able to bring deliverance and peace to a family.

"My husband is experiencing 'heart attacks' that are very strange," the new wife explained to me one day after church. This was a fairly new family in our growing congregation. She continued with this shocking story: "He only has these attacks when he is here in our house. We believe that something is wrong. We have been told that every former owner of this house died of heart attacks in their forties!" This husband was in his mid-forties and was deeply concerned for his life. We promised to bring our Spiritual Warfare prayer team to their house that following week. We were totally unprepared for that experience.

As we entered the house we explained to our team and the residents that, "we are going to pray and anoint with oil in every room of your house. We are going to ask the Lord to cleanse your house and deliver you from these demonic heart attacks. We began to pray in every room. We did not sense anything strange or unusual until we climbed the stairs. The owners explained that sometimes they could hear strange sounds coming from their attic. We asked if we might enter that area for a time of prayer. We were given permission and each of us stooped and entered into the rather cramped attic. We began to pray and then we experienced an attack that none of us could possibly explain.

I could scarcely believe what was happening to me. I felt the symptoms of a heart attack! I had suffered some of those attacks a few years prior and it had required a surgical procedure at St. Vincent's hospital. I was shocked to discover that every person praying in the attic that night was experiencing the same symptoms. There were around eight people there that night and we were all clutching our chests in pain. We prayed as we had never prayed before. We began to rebuke the enemy in the name of Jesus and the Blood of Calvary. In a matter of minutes the battle was over and peace reigned in that attic and in all of our hearts. The battle was won! The house was cleansed. We all celebrated and praised our Great Deliverer. We had seen a miracle that night!

59

Winona's Almost Tragic Fall
in Jamaica

We were staying at the beautiful, but small, hotel called "Jamel Hotel," situated on the edge of the azure blue waters of the Caribbean in Priory, not far from Ocho Rios, Jamaica. The owners were our friends and we always looked forward to spending a few days there while we were ministering in neighboring towns and villages. This was before our churches and schools had been established in Jamaica.

One of our favorite places to hold services was in a nursing home which was located only a short distance from the Jamel Hotel. Everyone always enjoyed walking to the nursing home because of the rolling tides of that beautiful ocean. On this particular evening we had made an appointment with the officials of the nursing home that would allow us to visit every ward, where we would minister to some of the poorest patients in all of Jamaica. These were primarily charity patients and the facilities were extremely poor. Pastor Larry Renihan spoke of this place as an example of "Poverty in Paradise."

Many of the patients could be seen almost naked while others were sitting in the middle of bodily discharges. The odors were many times almost sickening to our young American guests. But, in spite of all the smells and poverty we would always be blessed by the smiles, handshakes and greetings of these poverty-stricken patients. It was a joy to hear them sing the familiar choruses and hymns of the church that were interspersed with "Amens" and "Hallelujahs!" They loved seeing the Americans, who would walk among them and give hugs and handshakes. It was also a blessing to share our testimonies, songs and, sometimes, skits with those precious saints. But, this night was different!

We were just beginning our worship services and were ministering to the patients who were assembled in the first ward near the entrance. We had experienced some distractions from a competing reggae band that was playing very loudly nearby. We were forced to wait until they had quieted down a bit before we could begin. Several of our leaders sensed that a spirit of voodoo was present there that night.

In Jamaica witchcraft is prevalent. This type of demon worship is called "Obia" on that island and was brought there from the Ivory Coast of Africa with the slaves that were brought there in the 16th Century. One of the customs even today is for Obia worshippers to cast spells, or curses, on people they dislike. Christian missionaries have to be very careful of some of the carvings and other souvenirs that are sold to tourists. Oftentimes the "Obia-Men" will pray a curse against missionaries and other disliked people. We were aware that we were in the presence of evil spirits that day.

Our young people were standing around among the patients. Winona was standing on a high cement porch that overlooked a cement patio. All of a sudden Winona fell from the platform and struck her head on the concrete floor. We were all shocked.

We raced to her side and discovered that, mysteriously, she had struck the very top of her head. That was such a mystery since it would have required a 180-degree fall in that short distance. Winona was semi-conscious and in deep pain. We did not know what to do since there were no medical facilities nearby that we trusted. We felt that the fall was not natural and that we must, first of all, begin to intercede with fervent prayer for my precious wife and special friend to that youth team.

The Lord seemed to speak to our "spirits" that we should take Winona back to the Jamel Hotel where she could lie down and rest. We partially carried her back to the hotel and made her a bed on the grass outside on the hotel lawn. We asked all of the teens and their leaders to come around Winona and lay hands on her and pray. She still was not conscious and there was a large swelling on top of her head. The pain was severe. We questioned as to whether we should try to locate a doctor or clinic. The Spirit indicated to us that we should pray. That prayer meeting was unforgettable! Those precious young Hoosiers laid hands on Mama-san and prayed with tears streaming down their faces. They prayed with such intensity and faith. Finally, we felt the calmness of the Spirit surrounding us, and so we covered Winona in her sleeping bag and surrendered her to the Lord's safe-keeping. Several of the other teens and leaders decided to sleep outside with us that night. The air was refreshing and the ocean waves sounded so soothing. We all slept in peace and serenity. We were all resigned to the will of our loving Great Physician.

We awakened the next morning to find that the sun was shining. The birds were singing. The waves were crashing against the rocks and dock. Winona was gone! Her bed was empty! Where was Mama-san? Did something tragic happen during the night? Then, our concerns all melted and our hearts were filled with joy. Winona was up and preparing breakfast for all of her precious brood. We all celebrated as she showed us the place on her head where she had suffered a major blow. None of us could believe what we saw. We could find *no evidence* that she had suffered any damage to her head. There was no swelling or abrasions. There was no pain. We all celebrated that day. Every young American and adult, that day, was totally aware of the enemy's power, but, also that "the one who is in you is greater than the one who is in the world" (1 John 4:4).

60

The Spirit of Suicide

During the time that we ministered at Christ Community Church in Lamong, Indiana, we were challenged by many forms of spiritual warfare. Thankfully, we had a team of Prayer Warriors who were willing to join us in combat against the enemy. Of course, it was imperative that this type of battle required prayer and fasting in preparation for such combat. On one occasion we faced a form of "enemy strongholds" that was new to all of us.

A young couple with two sons informed us that they were facing a battle in their home that had them baffled. "The boys keep telling us that they felt like committing suicide," the mother said. The boys were faithful in Sunday school and church service each week. They explained that these feelings of suicide were like voices speaking in their minds. We knew that something must be done. That type of prayer request could not be mentioned from the pulpit since the majority of the average churchgoers are not familiar or comfortable with that type of conversation. I felt that we should check the history of the house where they lived. Here is what we discovered.

The two-story house, located not far from Eagletown and Jolietville, was more than 70 years old and had been occupied by a number of owners and renters. People who had lived in that area for many years revealed that every male that had occupied that home had "committed suicide." We realized that this was the cause of the two young boys' suicidal thoughts and dreams.

A time for spiritual warfare and cleansing was set up and we went to that house that, obviously, was under the influence of wicked spiritual "strongholds." We all prayed, anointed each room with oil and rebuked the enemy that was trying to destroy that family. The prayer meeting and cleansing was a success. But, I realized on the way back to our little house in Lamong that I was in trouble. I began to suffer a very powerful physical and mental attack against my mind and body. I had made a mistake, in that it is so important to pray for each member of the team before leaving the battle site. Fortunately, I had Winona to anoint me and pray for my cleansing.

I am totally convinced that "our struggle is not against flesh and blood, but against the rulers, against the authorities, against the powers of this dark world and against the spiritual forces of evil in the heavenly realms" (Ephesians 6:12). St. Paul tells us to put on the full armor of God, with the shield of faith and the sword of the Spirit, then to pray! (Ephesians 6:11–18) I pray that each of you will claim your victory and be "more than conquerors" against the world, the flesh and the devil (Romans 8:37).

61

The Witch Doctor Healed Him?

One of the most shocking revelations that I ever experienced was learning how powerful witchcraft and demon worship could be. I had never been taught much about that in Bible College and I was unprepared for the many attacks that we would suffer in the future ministries in America, Chile, Bolivia, Jamaica, Haiti and other countries. One evening I received a powerful and awakening experience.

I was walking along a country road in Bolivia that led to the house of some sick people who needed my attention. I had prepared injections of penicillin and other medications to help them through their sicknesses. While walking toward the patient's small cottage I passed a female witch doctor. This form of Satanism is called "Brujaria" in Bolivia and dates back to the early days of the Incas and other Indian tribes. After I had taken about twenty steps past the "Bruja" I felt a very powerful chill come all over my body. I turned to see that the witch doctor was placing a curse upon me.

From that moment on I was very much aware of the spiritual warfare that we were facing and I increased my prayers and spiritual warfare strategies. Some time after that we were called to sit with an expectant mother who knew that the "Bruja" was going to kill her new baby. Winona spent hours watching and praying as the young mother gave life to a baby girl. To our sadness the powers of darkness were able to penetrate the scene and take the life of the new baby. We knew that we must intensify our faith and warfare to overcome these dark forces that had ruled in this region for centuries. This was the best training that we had ever received and it has been a vital asset to our ministries ever since. But, there was one more episode that continues to mystify us. It happened to a man with a broken femur.

158

I had been called to examine a man who had broken his large upper leg femur bone. When I entered his tiny bedroom I realized that his situation was very serious. His broken leg was swollen horribly and the man's fever was very high. He was in excruciating pain and asked me what I could do for his leg. I gave him some antibiotics for the infection plus some pain medications and told him that we must take him to the Seventh Day Adventist Hospital located some 45 miles from our community. He refused to take my advice and said, "I will call the Brujo!"

I was totally certain that the man must have hospital treatment. I was wrong! During the night the Brujo came and cast some spells and incantations over the man and he was healed. I am still flabbergasted by that episode, but also aware that "our enemy" is powerful and like the priests of Pharoah, they too were able through witchcraft to do many of the same miracles that Moses did.

We must not take Satan lightly. Jesus warned us in Matthew 24:24 that "false Christs and false prophets will appear and perform great signs and miracles." He warned us not to be deceived, because Satan is powerful and we must learn to "put on the whole armor of God" with the sword of the Spirit and then pray in the Spirit! (Ephesians 6:11–18)

Let me encourage each of you to become a prayer warrior and to become "more than conquerors" over the world, the flesh and the devil! Amen!

62

The Drunken Sailor
Attacked Me!

In 1954 Winona and I were living in Arica, the northernmost port city of Chile, South America. This city was located on the edges of the Pacific Ocean and the Atacamba Desert, the driest desert in the world. We lived there for more than one year while working with Youth for Christ. Our mission was to evangelize and open churches in that region which later became part of the Church of the Nazarene. In the early days we faced a number of oppositions and attacks from the enemy.

At first we could find no place to purchase land or build a church. Next, our resident missionary family, the Boyd and Neva Skinner family, had to leave Chile. At that time we were still unable to speak the Spanish language. Pastor Carlyle McFarland, his wife Regina and their small daughter were there with us, but we did not know what we could do. Brother Carlyle and I decided to pray every evening in the desert until God would show us how we could minister to the people there. After forty nights the desert shook one night as if a heavy earthquake had struck. We were totally shaken by that powerful moment. The next service that we held I was able to speak for the first time in Spanish to a local congregation. I have always felt that this was a miracle.

There were other tests and trials in those early days, as the enemy did his best to defeat and discourage us. Because of some other problems, Winona and I were compelled to move into a tiny Sunday school room at the church. While we were living there our son Stephen was born. I took Winona to the hospital, but the doctor never showed up for the delivery and I was forced to deliver Stephen. This proved to be a great blessing. We were aware that the enemy was behind all of those trials. But, God used them to strengthen us for greater challenges in the future and He was teaching us how to do Spiritual Warfare. One day I faced one of the biggest battles I had ever known.

The McFarlands and my family were sitting in a small tea shop on the main street in Arica. This tea shop was close to the church where we lived. It was during moments like these that we became acquainted with local leaders and, also, we could practice our Spanish. One afternoon while we having a cup of tea an Italian sailor entered the café and began cursing me. We realized that he was from a ship that was anchored in the harbor and that he was drunk. He was a muscular sailor and he stood over me cursing and yelling at me. I did not understand everything that he said or why he was angry with me. I was told later that he did not like Americans and especially me. I did not know what to do. I had never seen the sailor before and I did not know enough Italian to reason with him. So, I stood up and quietly left the tea shop. The angry sailor followed me out into the street.

By this time a small crowd had gathered. Everyone was shocked by the screaming, cursing sailor. I continued walking away in the direction of our tiny apartment. He followed me as I crossed the street. I was totally embarrassed. I refused to retaliate in any form. I think that I was praying silently for directions and protection from the Lord. Then the situation worsened.

Mrs. Regina McFarland, wife of my missionary friend, Carlyle, decided to confront the angry, drunken sailor. She moved into his face and grabbed him by the shirt and said in English, "You leave this man alone!" That opened the door for an even greater attack. The sailor shoved Sister McFarland out of his presence. Then, Carlyle jumped on the sailor's back and wrapped his arms around his neck. The big, rough sailor jerked his head backwards into Carlyle's face knocking him to the street. Then, it was just me and him standing there in the street. I felt a powerful compulsion that was inexplicable. I always felt that ministers must turn the other cheek. That day the Lord led me to "put on the whole armor of God" and to do battle against this drunken, demon-crazed sailor.

In a matter of moments I saw myself giving that sailor a whipping there on the streets of Arica in front of a lot of people. After I had punched him a few times with strength that was from above, I believe, the sailor, who now had a ripped shirt and some bruises, began to run away. Soon the battle had ended and peace reigned on the street and around the tea shop. I examined Regina and Carlyle and they were not seriously injured. The spectators seemed to applaud the missionaries who at first had turned the other cheek and then took Moses' rod of correction and publicly spanked that sailor.

I walked to our little Sunday school room apartment and sat down in a church pew nearby. I began to sob and pray to the Lord. I asked God to forgive me if I had sinned. I'm sure I prayed for the drunken sailor. I prayed that the example we had shown that day would not be used of the enemy. I think that I learned one of the best spiritual warfare strategies of my life.

There are times when, like Jesus, we patiently endure criticism, insults, threats and other attacks. Sometimes I have allowed people to physically slap me. However, the greatest lesson that I learned that day is this: "Listen and obey the voice of the Shepherd." I love the Master as He endures the slaps, the curses, the nails, the whips and the cross. I love Him, also, when He enters the temple and literally whips the vendors out of His Father's house.

Perhaps there will be a time when each of us must stand up against the devil and his demons as they come to steal and kill us and our friends. Sometimes we have to respond like David against the Goliaths in our lives. Just listen and obey His voice and you will be "more than conquerors." It's all a matter of listening and responding!

Jack and Winona Terry
211 Crossbow Street
Sheridan, Indiana 46069
winonaterry@msn.com
Phone: (317) 663-4602